The Psalms Project Volume Three

Discovering the Spiritual World through the Psalms – Psalm 21 to 30

Michael Harvey Koplitz

All Scripture quotations, unless otherwise noted, are taken from the New American Standard Bible®, Copyright © 1960, 1962, 1963, 1968, 1971, 1972, 1973, 1975, 1977, 1995 by the Lockman Foundation. Used by permission (www.Lockman.org)

The NASB uses italic to indicate words that have been added for clarification. Citations are shown with large capital letters.

TABLE OF CONTENTS

The goal of this project:

This research project will examine the 150 psalms for the spiritual awareness each Psalm offers. Each Psalm will be examined by its language and the commentary of the Sages. The spiritual awareness analysis will be done in alignment with Ari's definition of the Tree of life, the Book of Creation, and the Zohar. Each verse of the Psalm will be rewritten using the intent of the language and spiritual commentary to convey its spiritual lesson.

The main resources:

The Zohar

The Book of Creation

Ari's writing on the Tree of Life and the Ten Sefirot

The Theological Wordbook of the Old Testament

Samson Hirsch's commentary on the Psalms

Tehillim – Psalms – A new translation with a commentary anthologized from the Talmudic and rabbinic sources

Accordance Bible Software

Psalm 21

New American Standard 1995	Hebrew
Psa. 21:0 For the choir director. A Psalm of David. **Psa. 21:1** O LORD, in Your strength the King will *be glad, And in Your [1]salvation how greatly he will rejoice! [2] You have *given him his heart's desire, And You have not withheld the request of his lips. [1]Selah. [3] For You *meet him with the blessings of good things; You set a *crown of fine gold on his head. [4] He asked life of You, You *gave it to him, *Length of days forever and ever. [5] His *glory is great through Your [1]salvation, *Splendor and majesty You place upon him. [6] For You make him [1]most *blessed forever; You make him joyful *with gladness in Your presence. **Psa. 21:7** For the King *trusts in the LORD, And through the lovingkindness of the Most High *he will not be shaken. [8] Your hand will *find out all your enemies;	לַמְנַצֵּחַ מִזְמוֹר Psa. 21:1 לְדָוִד ׃ ² יְהוָֹה בְּעָזְּךָ יִשְׂמַח־ מֶלֶךְ וּבִישׁוּעָתְךָ מַה־יָּגֶיל [יָּגֶל] מְאֹד ׃ ³ תַּאֲוַת לִבּוֹ נָתַתָּה לּוֹ וַאֲרֶשֶׁת שְׂפָתָיו בַּל־מָנַעְתָּ סֶּלָה ׃ ⁴ כִּי־ תְקַדְּמֶנּוּ בִּרְכוֹת טוֹב תָּשִׁית לְרֹאשׁוֹ עֲטֶרֶת פָּז ׃ ⁵ חַיִּים ׀ שָׁאַל מִמְּךָ נָתַתָּה לּוֹ אֹרֶךְ יָמִים עוֹלָם וָעֶד ׃ ⁶ גָּדוֹל כְּבוֹדוֹ בִּישׁוּעָתֶךָ הוֹד וְהָדָר תְּשַׁוֶּה עָלָיו ׃ ⁷ כִּי־תְשִׁיתֵהוּ בְרָכוֹת לָעַד תְּחַדֵּהוּ בְשִׂמְחָה אֶת־פָּנֶיךָ ׃ ⁸ כִּי־ הַמֶּלֶךְ בֹּטֵחַ בַּיהוָה וּבְחֶסֶד עֶלְיוֹן בַּל־יִמּוֹט ׃ ⁹ תִּמְצָא יָדְךָ לְכָל־אֹיְבֶיךָ יְמִינְךָ תִּמְצָא שֹׂנְאֶיךָ ׀ ¹⁰ תְּשִׁיתֵמוֹ

Your right hand will find out those who hate you.

9 You will make them [a]as a fiery oven in the time [1]of your anger;

The LORD will [b]swallow them up in His wrath,

And [c]fire will devour them.

10 Their [1]offspring You will destroy from the earth,

And their [2a]descendants from among the sons of men.

11 Though they [1a]intended evil against You

And [b]devised a plot,

They will not succeed.

12 For You will [a]make them turn their back;

You will [1]aim [b]with Your bowstrings at their faces.

13 Be exalted, O LORD, in Your strength;

We will [a]sing and praise Your power.

כְּתַנּוּר אֵשׁ לְעֵת פָּנֶיךָ יְהוָה
בְּאַפּוֹ יְבַלְּעֵם וְתֹאכְלֵם אֵשׁ:
11 פִּרְיָמוֹ מֵאֶרֶץ תְּאַבֵּד
וְזַרְעָם מִבְּנֵי אָדָם: 12 כִּי־נָטוּ
עָלֶיךָ רָעָה חָשְׁבוּ מְזִמָּה
בַּל־יוּכָלוּ: 13 כִּי תְּשִׁיתֵמוֹ
שֶׁכֶם בְּמֵיתָרֶיךָ תְּכוֹנֵן עַל־
פְּנֵיהֶם: 14 רוּמָה יְהוָה בְּעֻזֶּךָ
נָשִׁירָה וּנְזַמְּרָה גְּבוּרָתֶךָ:

References

Psalm 21:3 [a]Ps 59:10 [b]2 Sam 12:30	**Psalm 21:11** [1]Lit *stretched out* [a]Ps 2:1-3 [b]Ps 10:2
Psalm 21:4 [a]Ps 61:6; 133:3 [b]Ps 91:16	**Psalm 21:12** [1]Lit *make ready* [a]Ps 18:40 [b]Ps 7:12, 13
Psalm 21:5 [1]Or *victory* [a]Ps 9:14; 20:5 [b]Ps 8:5; 96:6	**Psalm 21:13** [a]Ps 59:16; 81:1
Psalm 21:6 [1]Lit *blessings* [a]1 Chr 17:27 [b]Ps 43:4	
Psalm 21:7 [a]Ps 125:1 [b]Ps 112:6	
Psalm 21:8 [a]Is 10:10	
Psalm 21:9 [1]Or *of your presence* [a]Mal 4:1 [b]Lam 2:2 [c]Ps 50:3	
Psalm 21:10 [1]Lit *fruit* [2]Lit *seed* [a]Ps 37:28	

Targum

Psa. 21:1 For praise; a psalm of David. [2] O LORD, in your strength the King Messiah will rejoice, and how greatly will he exult in your redemption! [3] You have given him the desire of his soul; and you have not withheld the expression of his lips forever. [4] For you will make good blessings go before him; you will place on his head a crown of refined gold. [5] Eternal life he asked of you; you gave him length of days forever and ever. [6] Great is his glory in your redemption; praise and splendor you will place on him. [7] Because you will give him blessings forever; you will gladden him with the gladness that is from your presence. [8] Because the King Messiah hopes in the LORD; and through the favor of the Most High he is not shaken. [9] The blow of your hand will reach all your foes; the vengeance of your right hand will find all your enemies. [10] You will make them like a fiery furnace at the time of your anger, O LORD; in his anger he will swallow them up and the inferno of Gehenna will consume them. [11] You will make their children perish from the earth, and their progeny from the sons of men. [12] Because they plotted evil against you, they thought evil thoughts, but they could not prevail against you. [13] Because for your people you made them one porter in the ropes of your tabernacle; you will prepare their way before them. [14] Stand up, O LORD, in your might; let us sing praise and dance in your strength.

Spiritual Awareness

The spiritual rewrite for the verses is in bold.

Introduction

This Psalm is dedicated to David and the Messiah. Each suffers from enemies who want to deny them their sovereignty. David was taunted by those who rebelled after his affair with Bathsheba. The Messiah will suffer at the hands of Gog and Magog. The Messiah will have wisdom greater than King Solomon and teach the nation and guide them back to the LORD.

Superscript

לַמְנַצֵּחַ (lam'nazecha) – the English translations of this Psalm like to use the phrase "for the choir director," however this translation is inaccurate. The "Theological Wordbook of the Old Testament" indicates that this translation is far from correct. A proper translation is "To Netzach." The Sefirah Netzach offers victory when its light is placed upon a person. The implication is that the people are happy that David had so many military victories. When David was victorious, the people were protected and prospered. The people are offering this prayer about David and their allegiance to him and the Sefirot Netzach.

To the Sefirah Netzach, a psalm of David.

Verse One

בְּעָזְּךָ (b'az'cha) – "in Your strength." This word also signified that David could withstand any attack. He had the strength of the LORD with him. At crucial moments in his life, the LORD gave him יְשׁוּעָה (yᵉshuʼâ) salvation. With the LORD at his side, David rejoiced, knowing that the Sefirah Netzach was with him. The Christian church holds this Psalm as a messianic prophecy because the name of the Messiah is in the verse.

O LORD, in your strength, the King rejoices, and from your salvation, the power of Netzach he exults.

Verse Two

The LORD gave David everything that he yearned for in his heart.

You have given him everything that he yearned for and gave him what his lips spoke. Meditate on this verse.

Verse Three

The LORD willed David to be the King of Israel. David was given the finest of blessings of good fortune.

You made him the King of Israel and gave him good fortune.

Verse Four

David asked the LORD for a life to be charged with a part of the divine plan. He sought to do the work of the LORD. It was a calling that went beyond his existence. David also asked for a calling that reached far beyond his own life. He asked for the LORD's plan to include his descendants.

He asked for life, and you gave it to him; a length of days and a future destiny.

Verse Five

Through the salvation of the LORD, David was able to win battles against the LORD's enemies and thus increased his honor and majesty. David called upon the Sefirah Hod for the LORD's splendor and majesty through his victories on the battlefield.

The Sefirah Hod bestowed splendor and majesty upon him through Your salvation.

Verse Six

David's Psalms have become a spiritual blessing to the people of the world. The Psalms are a part of the promise that the LORD gave to Abraham that the people of the world would be blessed through him.

For You appointed him for blessings for the distant future; You made him shine with gladness in the LORD's sovereignty.

Verse Seven

David acknowledges that his faith in the LORD is a part of the fulfillment of his being the King.

The King trusts in the LORD, and because of the blessings from the Sefirah Chesed, he will not waver.

Verse Eight

The hand of the LORD will intervene when necessary to chastise and discipline. The Sefirah Gevurah brings justice to the world. Thus it can be said that the hand of the LORD is the action of Gevurah.

The Sefirah Gevurah will find your enemies. Your right hand will overtake all who hate You.

Verse Nine

Malachi 3:19 portrays the future as a glowing oven in which the wicked will be destroyed. The wicked have helped prepare the righteous for the day of the final Tikkun. The LORD will cleanse the world of the wicked, leaving the righteous. The righteous are easy to find because the wicked stand out because of their sins.

You will make the wicked as a fiery oven at the Tikkun. The LORD will let them perish in His anger, and the fire of the oven will devour them.

Verse Ten

The LORD will not allow the children of the wicked to be born. Their descendants will pay for the deeds of the wicked.

You will cause their fruit to vanish from the earth and their seed from among the children of men.

Verse Eleven

כִּי־נָטוּ עָלֶיךָ (kee – natoo alecha) – means "intended evil against." This phrase expresses the intention to cause an inevitable fate to overtake another person. Wicked people plan to do evil against the LORD. The LORD will not allow the plan to come to be.

For they intended evil against You; they devised a plan, but they will fail.

Verse Twelve

For you will make them turn their backs; you will aim your bowstrings at their faces.

Verse Thirteen

It must be remembered that it is the LORD's omnipotence that we can recognize.

You are invincible, LORD, as seen through Your strength. We will proclaim You in song and sing of it.

Psalm 22

New American Standard 1995	Hebrew

Psa. 22:1 [a]My God, my God, why have You forsaken me?

[1][b]Far from my deliverance are the words of my [2][c]groaning.

2 O my God, I [a]cry by day, but You do not answer;

And by night, but [1]I have no rest.

3 Yet [a]You are holy,

O You who [1]are enthroned upon [b]the praises of Israel.

4 In You our fathers [a]trusted;

They trusted and You [b]delivered them.

5 To You they cried out and were delivered;

[a]In You they trusted and were not [1]disappointed.

Psa. 22:6 But I am a [a]worm and not a man,

A [b]reproach of men and [c]despised by the people.

7 All who see me [1][a]sneer at me;

They [2]separate with the lip, they [b]wag the head, *saying,*

8 "[1]Commit *yourself* to the LORD; [a]let Him deliver him;

Let Him rescue him, because He delights in him."

Psa. 22:9 Yet You are He who [a]brought me forth from the womb;

You made me trust *when* upon my mother's breasts.

10 Upon You I was cast [a]from [1]birth;

לַמְנַצֵּחַ עַל־אַיֶּלֶת הַשַּׁחַר מִזְמוֹר
לְדָוִד ׃ 2 אֵלִי אֵלִי לָמָה עֲזַבְתָּנִי
3 רָחוֹק מִישׁוּעָתִי דִּבְרֵי שַׁאֲגָתִי ׃
אֱלֹהַי אֶקְרָא יוֹמָם וְלֹא תַעֲנֶה
וְלַיְלָה וְלֹא־דוּמִיָּה לִי ׃ 4 וְאַתָּה
קָדוֹשׁ יוֹשֵׁב תְּהִלּוֹת יִשְׂרָאֵל ׃ 5 בְּךָ
6 בָּטְחוּ אֲבֹתֵינוּ בָּטְחוּ וַתְּפַלְּטֵמוֹ ׃
אֵלֶיךָ זָעֲקוּ וְנִמְלָטוּ בְּךָ בָטְחוּ
וְלֹא־בוֹשׁוּ ׃ 7 וְאָנֹכִי תוֹלַעַת וְלֹא־
אִישׁ חֶרְפַּת אָדָם וּבְזוּי עָם ׃ 8 כָּל־
רֹאַי יַלְעִגוּ לִי יַפְטִירוּ בְשָׂפָה יָנִיעוּ
רֹאשׁ ׃ 9 גֹּל אֶל־יְהוָה יְפַלְּטֵהוּ
יַצִּילֵהוּ כִּי חָפֵץ בּוֹ ׃ 10 כִּי־אַתָּה
גֹחִי מִבָּטֶן מַבְטִיחִי עַל־שְׁדֵי אִמִּי ׃
11 עָלֶיךָ הָשְׁלַכְתִּי מֵרָחֶם מִבֶּטֶן אִמִּי
אֵלִי אָתָּה ׃ 12 אַל־תִּרְחַק מִמֶּנִּי כִּי־
13 צָרָה קְרוֹבָה כִּי־אֵין עוֹזֵר ׃
סְבָבוּנִי פָּרִים רַבִּים אַבִּירֵי בָשָׁן
כִּתְּרוּנִי ׃ 14 פָּצוּ עָלַי פִּיהֶם אַרְיֵה
טֹרֵף וְשֹׁאֵג ׃ 15 כַּמַּיִם נִשְׁפַּכְתִּי
וְהִתְפָּרְדוּ כָּל־עַצְמוֹתָי הָיָה לִבִּי
כַּדּוֹנָג נָמֵס בְּתוֹךְ מֵעָי ׃ 16 יָבֵשׁ
כַּחֶרֶשׂ ׀ כֹּחִי וּלְשׁוֹנִי מֻדְבָּק
מַלְקוֹחָי וְלַעֲפַר־מָוֶת תִּשְׁפְּתֵנִי ׃ 17
כִּי סְבָבוּנִי כְּלָבִים עֲדַת מְרֵעִים

You have been my God from my mother's womb.

Psa. 22:11   *a*Be not far from me, for [1]trouble is near;

For there is *b*none to help.

12   Many *a*bulls have surrounded me; Strong *bulls* of *b*Bashan have encircled me.

13   They *a*open wide their mouth at me,

As a ravening and a roaring *b*lion.

14   I am *a*poured out like water, And all my *b*bones are out of joint; My *c*heart is like wax; It is melted within [1]me.

15   My *a*strength is dried up like a potsherd, And *b*my tongue cleaves to my jaws; And You *c*lay me [1]in the dust of death.

16   For *a*dogs have surrounded me; [1]A band of evildoers has encompassed me; [2]They *b*pierced my hands and my feet.

17   I can count all my bones. *a*They look, they stare at me;

18   They *a*divide my garments among them, And for my clothing they cast lots.

Psa. 22:19   But You, O LORD, *a*be not far off; O You my help, *b*hasten to my assistance.

20   Deliver my [1]soul from *a*the sword, My *b*only *life* from the [2]power of the dog.

21   Save me from the *a*lion's mouth;

הֱקִיפוּנִי כָּאֲרִי יָדַי וְרַגְלָי ׃ 18
אֲסַפֵּר כָּל־עַצְמוֹתָי הֵמָּה יַבִּיטוּ
יִרְאוּ־בִי ׃ 19 יְחַלְּקוּ בְגָדַי לָהֶם
וְעַל־לְבוּשִׁי יַפִּילוּ גוֹרָל ׃ 20 וְאַתָּה
יְהוָה אַל־תִּרְחָק אֱיָלוּתִי לְעֶזְרָתִי
חוּשָׁה ׃ 21 הַצִּילָה מֵחֶרֶב נַפְשִׁי
מִיַּד־כֶּלֶב יְחִידָתִי ׃ 22 הוֹשִׁיעֵנִי
מִפִּי אַרְיֵה וּמִקַּרְנֵי רֵמִים עֲנִיתָנִי ׃
אֲסַפְּרָה שִׁמְךָ לְאֶחָי בְּתוֹךְ קָהָל 23
אֲהַלְלֶךָּ ׃ 24 יִרְאֵי יְהוָה הַלְלוּהוּ
כָּל־זֶרַע יַעֲקֹב כַּבְּדוּהוּ וְגוּרוּ
מִמֶּנּוּ כָּל־זֶרַע יִשְׂרָאֵל ׃ 25 כִּי לֹא־
בָזָה וְלֹא שִׁקַּץ עֱנוּת עָנִי וְלֹא־
הִסְתִּיר פָּנָיו מִמֶּנּוּ וּבְשַׁוְּעוֹ אֵלָיו
שָׁמֵעַ ׃ 26 מֵאִתְּךָ תְהִלָּתִי בְּקָהָל רָב
נְדָרַי אֲשַׁלֵּם נֶגֶד יְרֵאָיו ׃ 27 יֹאכְלוּ
עֲנָוִים וְיִשְׂבָּעוּ יְהַלְלוּ יְהוָה
דֹּרְשָׁיו יְחִי לְבַבְכֶם לָעַד ׃ 28 יִזְכְּרוּ
וְיָשֻׁבוּ אֶל־יְהוָה כָּל־אַפְסֵי־אָרֶץ
וְיִשְׁתַּחֲווּ לְפָנֶיךָ כָּל־מִשְׁפְּחוֹת
גוֹיִם ׃ 29 כִּי לַיהוָה הַמְּלוּכָה וּמֹשֵׁל
בַּגּוֹיִם ׃ 30 אָכְלוּ וַיִּשְׁתַּחֲווּ כָּל־
דִּשְׁנֵי־אֶרֶץ לְפָנָיו יִכְרְעוּ כָּל־
יוֹרְדֵי עָפָר וְנַפְשׁוֹ לֹא חִיָּה ׃ 31 זֶרַע
יַעַבְדֶנּוּ יְסֻפַּר לַאדֹנָי לַדּוֹר ׃ 32
יָבֹאוּ וְיַגִּידוּ צִדְקָתוֹ לְעַם נוֹלָד כִּי
עָשָׂה ׃

From the horns of the [b]wild oxen You [c]answer me.

Psa. 22:22   I will [a]tell of Your name to my brethren;

In the midst of the assembly I will praise You.

23   [a]You who fear the LORD, praise Him;

All you [1]descendants of Jacob, [b]glorify Him,

And [c]stand in awe of Him, all you [1]descendants of Israel.

24   For He has [a]not despised nor abhorred the affliction of the afflicted;

Nor has He [b]hidden His face from him;

But [c]when he cried to Him for help, He heard.

Psa. 22:25   From You *comes* [a]my praise in the great assembly;

I shall [b]pay my vows before those who fear Him.

26   The [1]afflicted will eat and [a]be satisfied;

Those who seek Him will [b]praise the LORD.

Let your [c]heart live forever!

27   All the [a]ends of the earth will remember and turn to the LORD,

And all the [b]families of the nations will worship before [1]You.

28   For the [a]kingdom is the LORD'S

And He [b]rules over the nations.

29   All the [1a]prosperous of the earth will eat and worship,

All those who [b]go down to the dust will bow before Him,

Even he who [2c]cannot keep his soul alive.

30 [1][a]Posterity will serve Him; It will be told of the Lord to [b]the *coming* generation. **31** They will come and [a]will declare His righteousness To a people [b]who will be born, that He has performed *it*.	

30   [1][a]Posterity will serve Him;

References

Psalm 22:0

¹Lit *the hind of the morning*

Psalm 22:1

¹Or Why are You so *far from helping me,* and from *the words of my groaning?*
²Lit *roaring*
*ᵃ*Matt 27:46; Mark 15:34
*ᵇ*Ps 10:1
*ᶜ*Job 3:24; Ps 6:6; 32:3; 38:8

Psalm 22:2

¹Lit *there is no silence for me*
*ᵃ*Ps 42:3; 88:1

Psalm 22:3

¹Or *inhabit the praises*
*ᵃ*Ps 99:9
*ᵇ*Deut 10:21; Ps 148:14

Psalm 22:4

*ᵃ*Ps 78:53
*ᵇ*Ps 107:6

Psalm 22:5

¹Or *ashamed*
*ᵃ*Is 49:23

Psalm 22:6

*ᵃ*Job 25:6; Is 41:14
*ᵇ*Ps 31:11
*ᶜ*Is 49:7; 53:3

Psalm 22:7

¹Or *mock me*
²I.e. make mouths at me
*ᵃ*Ps 79:4; Is 53:3; Luke 23:35
*ᵇ*Matt 27:39; Mark 15:29

Psalm 22:8

¹Lit *Roll;* another reading is *He committed himself*
*ᵃ*Ps 91:14; Matt 27:43

Psalm 22:9

*ᵃ*Ps 71:5, 6

Psalm 22:10

¹Lit a *womb*
*ᵃ*Is 46:3; 49:1

Psalm 22:11

¹Or *distress*
*ᵃ*Ps 71:12
*ᵇ*2 Kin 14:26; Ps 72:12; Is 63:5

Psalm 22:12

*ᵃ*Ps 22:21; 68:30
*ᵇ*Deut 32:14; Amos 4:1

Psalm 22:13

*ᵃ*Job 16:10; Ps 35:21; Lam 2:16; 3:46
*ᵇ*Ps 10:9; 17:12

Psalm 22:14

¹Lit *my inward parts*
*ᵃ*Job 30:16
*ᵇ*Ps 31:10; Dan 5:6
*ᶜ*Josh 7:5; Job 23:16; Ps 73:26; Nah 2:10

Psalm 22:15

¹Lit *to*
*ᵃ*Ps 38:10
*ᵇ*John 19:28
*ᶜ*Ps 104:29

Psalm 22:16
[1]Or *An assembly*
[2]Another reading is *Like a lion, my...*
[a]Ps 59:6, 7
[b]Matt 27:35; John 20:25

Psalm 22:17
[a]Luke 23:27, 35

Psalm 22:18
[a]Matt 27:35; Mark 15:24; Luke 23:34; John 19:24

Psalm 22:19
[a]Ps 22:11
[b]Ps 70:5

Psalm 22:20
[1]Or *life*
[2]Lit *paw*
[a]Ps 37:14
[b]Ps 35:17

Psalm 22:21
[a]Ps 22:13
[b]Ps 22:12
[c]Ps 34:4; 118:5; 120:1

Psalm 22:22
[a]Ps 40:10; Heb 2:12

Psalm 22:23
[1]Lit *seed*
[a]Ps 135:19, 20
[b]Ps 86:12
[c]Ps 33:8

Psalm 22:24
[a]Ps 69:33
[b]Ps 27:9; 69:17; 102:2
[c]Ps 31:22; Heb 5:7

Psalm 22:25
[a]Ps 35:18; 40:9, 10
[b]Ps 61:8; Eccl 5:4

Psalm 22:26
[1]Or *poor*
[a]Ps 107:9
[b]Ps 40:16
[c]Ps 69:32

Psalm 22:27
[1]Some versions read *Him*
[a]Ps 2:8; 82:8
[b]Ps 86:9

Psalm 22:28
[a]Ps 47:7; Obad 21; Zech 14:9; Matt 6:13
[b]Ps 47:8

Psalm 22:29
[1]Lit *fat ones*
[2]Or *did not*
[a]Ps 17:10; 45:12; Hab 1:16
[b]Ps 28:1; Is 26:19
[c]Ps 89:48

Psalm 22:30
[1]Lit *A seed*
[a]Ps 102:28
[b]Ps 102:18

Psalm 22:31
[a]Ps 40:9; 71:18
[b]Ps 78:6

Targum

Psa. 22:1 For praise; concerning the strength of the regular morning sacrifice; a psalm of David. [2] My God, my God, why have you left me far from my redemption? – are the words of my outcry. [3] O God, I call by day and you will not accept my prayer; and by night I have no quiet [4] But you are holy, who make the world rest on the psalms of Israel. [5] Our fathers hoped in you; they hoped in your word, and you saved them. [6] In your presence they prayed and were saved; and on you they relied, and were not disappointed. [7] But I am a feeble worm, not a rational man; the reproach of the sons of men, and the butt of the Gentiles. [8] All who see me will gloat over me, attacking with their lips; they will shake their heads. [9] Let him give praise in the presence of the LORD; and he has delivered him, he saved him because he favored him. [10] Because you took me out of the womb; you gave me hope on my mother's breasts. [11] By your aid I was pulled forth from [her] bowels; from my mother's womb you are my God. [12] Be not far from me, for trouble is near, for there is no redeemer. [13] The Gentiles have surrounded me, who are like many bulls; the princes of Mathnan have hemmed me in. [14] They open their mouths at me like a roaring and ravaging lion. [15] Like water I am poured out; all my bones are crushed; my heart is melting like wax within my bowels. [16] My strength has dried up like a potsherd, and my tongue is stuck to my palate; and you have brought me to the grave. [17] Because the wicked have surrounded me, who are like many dogs; a gathering of evildoers has hemmed me in, biting my hands and feet like a lion. [18] I will tell of all the wounds of my bones; those who see me despise me. [19] They divide my clothing for themselves; and for my cloak they will cast lots. [20] You, O LORD, do not be far off; O my strength, hurry to my aid. [21] Save my soul from those who slay with the sword; from the power of the dog [save] the breath of my body. [22] Redeem me from the mouth of the lion; and from kings who are strong and tall as a bull you have received my prayer. [23] I will tell of the might of your name to my brothers; in the midst of the assembly I will praise you. [24] O you who fear the LORD, sing praise in his presence; all the seed of Jacob, give him glory; and be afraid of him, all you seed of Israel. [25] For he does not despise or scorn the prayer of the poor; and he has not removed his presence from their midst; and when they pray in his presence, he accepts [their prayer]. [26] My psalm in the assembly of many people is from you; I will fulfill my vows before those who fear him. [27] The humble will eat and be satisfied; those who seek the LORD will sing praise in his presence; the spirit of prophecy will dwell in the thoughts of your hearts forever. [28] All the ends of the earth will remember his offerings and will repent in the presence of the LORD; and all the families of the Gentiles will bow down before you. [29] For kingship is from the presence of the LORD, and he rules over the Gentiles. [30] All who are fat on earth have eaten and bowed down; all who descend to the grave prostrate themselves before him; but the soul of the wicked shall not live. [31] The seed of Abraham will worship in his presence; and they will tell the mighty greatness of the

LORD to a later generation. [32] Their children will return and recount his generosity; to his people yet to be born [they will recount] the wonders he performed.

Spiritual Awareness

Introduction

This Psalm of David deals with events destined to occur hundreds of years after David's time. He foresaw the bleak future of the Babylonian and Persian exiles. He also saw the threat of Haman and Ahasuerus against the Hebrew nation. This Psalm may have been dedicated to Queen Esther, who was the savior of the people.

When David fled from Absolom, Shimi ben Gera of the tribe of Benjamin viciously cursed David. When David's men caught him, he did not allow them to kill him. The Talmud Megilla 13a says that David foresaw that Mordecai and Esther were descendants of Shimi. For the sake of the future of David's people, he did not execute Shimi even though he had reasonable cause to do so.

Due to the length of this Psalm, a complete spiritual awareness rewrite was not done. The spiritual awareness of each verse is brought out in the analysis.

Superscript

עַל־אַיֶּלֶת הַשַּׁחַר (al-ayelet hashachar) – translated means "upon the morning star." This phrase refers to the first visible light before the sunrise. It could have been the title of the Psalm. The English translation in the NASB 1995 is a name being assumed to be that of the choir director. Rabbi Hirsch uses the translation "upon the strengthening power of day's dawning." This Psalm thus sings of the renewed vigor which a man may derive from the knowledge that the morning brings and is not too far away.

לַמְנַצֵּחַ (lam'natzecha) – translation is "choirmaster." However, it is also a call to the Sefirah Netzach. The spiritual awareness translation is "to the Sefirah Netzach who grants victory."

Verse one

David realizes that Israel's disloyalty to the LORD's Law was sufficient reason for the pain that the nation did endure (for David, it was a future of endurance of pain). Even though the LORD allowed the Assyrians and Babylonians to attack and destroy the northern ten tribes, He kept His covenant.

> [44] 'Yet in spite of this, when they are in the land of their enemies, I will not reject them, nor will I so abhor them as to destroy them, breaking My covenant with them; for I am the LORD their God. (Leviticus 26:44)

David thus had a prophecy or a vision from the LORD of the future of His people.

Verse two

David's prayer for the future did not have the desired effect. It was disturbing to know this future, and it kept him up at night worrying and praying for his people.

Verse three

קָדוֹשׁ (kadosh) – means "holy." In this Psalm, this word has a deeper spiritual meaning. It is a force that is far beyond any other force in the Universe. It only belongs to the LORD. Israel is the sole spiritual bearer of kadosh's divine revelation. It is a force for the benefit of all humanity once all humanity recognizes the presence and love of the LORD

Verse four and five

Our fathers called out to the LORD and placed their faith and trust in You. In the past, LORD, you delivered them from danger. They felt reborn and had a new and better life in their arms. If you have not placed your complete faith and trust in the LORD, you can do it anytime; why not now? David realized that His faith and trust in the LORD enriched his life. He was sure that the LORD would deliver his people from the anguish of captivity and exile.

Verse six

David called himself a worm because he was scorned by men and despised among the nations that surrounded him. The revolt against David was in progress, and he had to flee into the mountains. He felt like an outlaw in his own country.

Verse seven

David refers to the people who felt that he was unworthy and would not look at his face. The people in the revolt did not want to see him alive.

Verse eight

David is expressing his inner feeling. Is he praying for the salvation of the people who want to kill him? Perhaps and if so, he is telling his enemies that they will see the ways of the LORD and come into faith and trust. If that happened, they would have stopped fighting David and instead installed him on the throne of Israel and protected him and his interests.

Verse nine and ten

The birth of the nation of Israel came to be through the favor and direction of the LORD. Up to this point (of David's reign), Israel's history was filled with difficulties and misery. So many nations of the world disappeared from history due to hardship, especially from neighbors. The LORD instructed Abraham to leave his home and extended family to travel and settle in Canaan, which was not that hospitable at the time. Since the LORD was with Abraham, he was able to establish his family there. David acknowledged this fact. Suppose the LORD did not intervene and had not gotten Joseph sent to Egypt, the family would have died of starvation. After the Egyptians decided to enslave the nation of Israel, the LORD sent Moses to rescue them. The hand of the LORD gave victory to Joshua and his army during the conquest of Canaan. The hand of the LORD was with David even in the turbulent years.

Verse eleven

David knew that he was in trouble, and he needed the hand of the LORD upon him more than ever. He felt that he had no earthly help.

Verse twelve and thirteen

פָּרִים (gareem) – translated as "bull." This term is usually employed to describe the power of nations. These verses are referring to the nations that surrounded David. These nations did not necessarily agree with each other. However, there was one thing they did agree on: they hated the Hebrew people. They acted as one mind to fight David.

Verse fourteen and fifteen

David felt that he was devoid of strength. Perhaps he tired of the continual fight against his enemies. To be poured out like water meant that he must conform to whatever future lied ahead of him in the same way water takes the shape of the cup or surface that it is poured out on.

Verse Sixteen

David continued to describe his problems by says that dogs have surrounded him. Perhaps it is because the dogs smelled defeat on David. The symbolism is that David felt defeated. The NASB 1995 translation of the last part of this verse is incorrect. The translation says, "They pierced my hands and my feet." The Hebrew word for piercing is not in this verse. Also, the word for lion, which is in Hebrew, is not in the English translation. The proper English translation is "like lions, at my hands and feet." The Targum supports the translation not having anything to do with piercing. The Christian Church has used this Psalm as a Messianic prophecy Psalm. It is not a Messianic prophecy Psalm when examined in its original language.

The Church used the Septuagint verse, which reads: "(21:16) For many dogs have compassed me: the assembly of the wicked doers has beset me round: they pierced my hands and my feet" (Source: https://biblehub.com/sep/psalms/22.htm). A newer English translation which is a bit closer to the Hebrew, can be found at: http://ccat.sas.upenn.edu/nets/edition/24-ps-nets.pdf

Therefore, the prophecy of Jesus of Nazareth having his hands and feet nailed is based on the Greek translation of the Hebrew Scriptures that was done around 225 BCE. Since the theological position of the Church is not based on the original material, it is incorrect to use Psalm 22 as a Messianic prophetic Psalm.

Verse seventeen

Rabbi Hirsch has an entirely different translation for this verse. His translation is: "I recount to myself that whichever was and still is my strength; they behold it and look at me." Thus this verse, in this form, says that Israel, amidst the dangers and perils that it will face (and did face) will nurture the memories of its past, which was filled and upheld by the LORD. The LORD will always be with His people no matter the situation.

Verse eighteen

David said that he would freely give his enemies his material possessions. Clothing was considered a valuable commodity at that time. David knew that the LORD would ensure that he had whatever he needed to survive. Therefore, it did not matter to David that his enemies were dividing his clothing. This is another verse that the Church uses to justify the Psalm as being a messianic prophecy. It is David telling the LORD that material possession is not essential when compared to the love of the LORD.

Verse nineteen

In verse sixteen, David spoke about the dogs who were going to attack him. Symbolically the dogs are the surrounding nations and those leading the revolt. It is a cry to the LORD for help.

Verse twenty

The power against David is in the nations that surround him and in the hands of his enemies.

Verse twenty-one

David asks the LORD to be saved from the fierce animals that lived in Judea, which David was asking for the LORD's protection from his enemies.

Verse twenty-two

David said to the LORD that he will tell the people of Israel about the LORD and continue praising Him.

Verse twenty-three

David reminds us that the people who show reverence to the LORD will always offer their praise and worship to Him.

Verse twenty-four

This is another reminder from David that in the darkest days of the dispersion of the people, the LORD will always be near then,

Verse twenty-five

Anytime that David honored someone, the LORD would be praised at the same time.

Verse twenty-six

People who love the LORD and praise him will live forever with Him.

Verse twenty-seven

The people who remain "humble" before the LORD and do not seek out power and glory for themselves will be known to Him.

Verse twenty-Eight

All the kingdoms on Earth belong to the LORD. One day they will all realize this and pay homage to Him.

Verse twenty-nine

A person has to submit to the LORD's will to enjoy the pleasures and delights that the Earth and the LORD offer.

Verse thirty

In David's day, he knew that his people dedicated their lives to the LORD. In the future, David envisioned all humanity praising the LORD. Unfortunately, that day is not today.

Verse thirty-one

The current generation of elders must pass down their knowledge of the LORD to the next generation. By doing this, the name and the works of the LORD will be preserved through all eternity.

Psalm 23

New American Standard 1995	Hebrew

Psa. 23:0 A Psalm of David.
 	
Psa. 23:1 The LORD is my [a]shepherd,
  I [1]shall [b]not want.
2 He makes me lie down in [a]green pastures;
  He [b]leads me beside [1c]quiet waters.
3 He [a]restores my soul;
  He [b]guides me in the [1c]paths of righteousness
  For His name's sake.
 	
Psa. 23:4 Even though I [a]walk through the [1]valley of the shadow of death,
  I [b]fear no [2]evil, for [c]You are with me;
  Your [d]rod and Your staff, they comfort me.
5 You [a]prepare a table before me in the presence of my enemies;
  You [1]have [b]anointed my head with oil;
  My [c]cup overflows.
6 [1]Surely [a]goodness and lovingkindness will follow me all the days of my life,
  And I will [2b]dwell in the house of the LORD [3]forever.
	‏1 מִזְמוֹר לְדָוִד יְהוָה רֹעִי לֹא
	אֶחְסָר׃ ‏2 בִּנְאוֹת דֶּשֶׁא יַרְבִּיצֵנִי
	עַל־מֵי מְנֻחוֹת יְנַהֲלֵנִי׃ ‏3 נַפְשִׁי
	יְשׁוֹבֵב יַנְחֵנִי בְמַעְגְּלֵי־צֶדֶק
	לְמַעַן שְׁמוֹ׃ ‏4 גַּם כִּי־אֵלֵךְ
	בְּגֵיא צַלְמָוֶת לֹא־אִירָא רָע
	כִּי־אַתָּה עִמָּדִי שִׁבְטְךָ
	וּמִשְׁעַנְתֶּךָ הֵמָּה יְנַחֲמֻנִי׃ ‏5
	תַּעֲרֹךְ לְפָנַי שֻׁלְחָן נֶגֶד צֹרְרָי
	דִּשַּׁנְתָּ בַשֶּׁמֶן רֹאשִׁי כּוֹסִי רְוָיָה׃
	‏6 אַךְ טוֹב וָחֶסֶד יִרְדְּפוּנִי כָּל־
	יְמֵי חַיָּי וְשַׁבְתִּי בְּבֵית־יְהוָה
	לְאֹרֶךְ יָמִים׃

References

<table>
<tr><td>

Psalm 23:1
[1]Or *do*
[a]Ps 78:52; 80:1; Is 40:11; Jer 31:10; Ezek 34:11-13; John 10:11; 1 Pet 2:25
[b]Ps 34:9, 10; Phil 4:19

Psalm 23:2
[1]Lit *waters of rest*
[a]Ps 65:11-13; Ezek 34:14
[b]Rev 7:17
[c]Ps 36:8; 46:4

Psalm 23:3
[1]Lit *tracks*
[a]Ps 19:7
[b]Ps 5:8; 31:3
[c]Ps 85:13; Prov 4:11; 8:20

Psalm 23:4
[1]Or *valley of deep darkness*
[2]Or *harm*
[a]Job 10:21, 22; Ps 107:14
[b]Ps 3:6; 27:1
[c]Ps 16:8; Is 43:2
[d]Mic 7:14

Psalm 23:5
[1]Or *anoint*
[a]Ps 78:19
[b]Ps 92:10; Luke 7:46
[c]Ps 16:5

</td><td>

Psalm 23:6
[1]Or *Only*
[2]Another reading is *return to*
[3]Lit *for length of days*
[a]Ps 25:7, 10
[b]Ps 27:4-6

</td></tr>
</table>

Targum

Psa. 23:1 A psalm of David. It is the LORD who fed his people in the wilderness; they did not lack anything. **2** In a place of thirst he will settle me in pleasant grass; he led me to the waters of rest. **3** He will restore my soul with manna; he led me in the paths of righteousness for the sake of his name. **4** Indeed, when I go into exile by the plain of the shadow of death, I will fear no evil; for your word is my help, your straight staff and your Torah, they will comfort me. **5** You have set before me a high table of manna in front of my oppressors; you have fattened my body with stuffed fowl, and with anointing oil [you have fattened] the heads of my priests; my goblet is wide. **6** Indeed grace and favor will follow me all the days of my life, while I sit in the sanctuary of the LORD for length of days.

Spiritual Awareness

The spiritual rewrite for the verses is in bold.

Introduction

David was being chased by Saul's men, who intended to kill him. For David, it was a dark and discouraging period in his life. He hid in the Hereth forest (1 Sam 22:5). This forest was a barren, desolate forest, parched and dry. The LORD did not abandon David. He soaked the dry forest with moisture that had the flavor of the world to come, making the grass and leaves of the forest succulent and edible (this can be found in the Midrash).

This psalm is customarily said between the washing of the hands and offering the blessing over the bread. This custom can be explained using Gematria. There are fifty-seven words in the psalm, the numerical equivalent to the word "nourishes." In addition, there are 227 letters in the psalm, which is equivalent to the word "blessing." Reciting and living by the words of this psalm offers a blessed life with ample provisions.

Verse One

מִזְמוֹר לְדָוִד (meez'mor l'david) – means "a psalm of David." This short superscript is not in the English versions of the psalm. The Hebrew and Targum verses do include it. This phrase is a part of verse one.

רֹעִי (roeer) – means "feed, pasture." Why does the NASB use the word "shepherd?" The English translations tend to use church-accepted language when there is a discrepancy. The Septuagint (LXX Brenton translation) says, "The Lord tends me as a shepherd, and I shall want nothing." This is probably where the shepherd language originated for the church. The Targum in English says, "It is the LORD who fed his people in the wilderness; they did not lack anything." The shepherd's job was to ensure that his flock of sheep was fed. Hirsch and Steinsaltz use the translation shepherd.

The translation from the Targum is a more accurate translation when it is read with the background of the Midrash. The LORD brought moisture and food to the Hereth forest so that David could survive. He needed food and water in this forest. Where was he going to find it? Since that was impossible, the LORD gave him the food and water he needed. The LORD did the same thing for the Israelites while they roamed in the desert of Sinai. The LORD brought moisture and manna from Heaven for the people. The custom of reciting the psalm between the washing of hands and the blessing over bread is a reminder of the miracle of manna and to remember that the LORD will provide the basic needs. David acknowledged the LORD's gifts to his ancestors and to him.

A psalm of David. It is the LORD who fed his people in the wilderness; they did not lack anything.

Verse two

בִּנְאוֹת (been'ot) – means "in the pastures." This word is derived from the Aramaic word for "beautiful, pleasant." An additional "vuv" is added to the Aramaic word, and the result is the word for "pleasant places, pastures." Therefore, the translation of "pleasant place" can be used. For a flock of sheep, a pleasant place is a pasture. The Targum adds the words "in a place of thirst." When the sheep move from an old water source to a new water source, they become thirsty. The shepherd is aware of this situation and knows where the water holes are and whether his sheep can reach them before they die from dehydration. The LORD made the Hereth forest a pleasant place for David by bringing water and food to him.

In my thirst, He will settle me in pleasant grass; he leads me to the peaceful waters to rest.

Verse three

נַפְשִׁי (naph'shee) – means "soul." This is a broad translation. In the spiritual understanding of the soul, there are five parts.

1. Nefesh
2. Ruach
3. Neshama
4. Chaya
5. Yechida

The Nefesh in the Kabbalah is considered the soul's flesh while in Malkhut (Earthly kingdom). Therefore, in this verse, the spiritual awareness is the understanding that the restoration of the soul is restoring David's body. He required food, water, and especially rest. He had been running away from Saul's troops and was exhausted when he reached the Hereth forest. The LORD rejuvenated his body with the three items already mentioned.

Using the Nefesh part of the soul, the spiritual awareness translation is:

Again and again, He gives my flesh food, water, and rest; He also leads me in the paths of righteous justice for His Name's sake.

Verse four

The shadow of death that David was walking through was his fleeing path from Saul. If the soldiers caught David, they would have murdered him on the spot. David placed his faith and trust in the LORD, knowing that the LORD would save him since he was anointed to be the next King of Israel.

When I go into exile through the valley overshadowed by death, I fear no evil because You are with me; Your rod and Your staff comfort me.

Verse five

David said that the LORD gives peace and inner calmness amid suffering. David felt safe in the Hereth forest because the LORD had led him there. He can enjoy the respite that he needed. This is what is meant by the phrase "you prepare a table before me in the presence of my enemy." The anointed is a reminder that Samuel anointed David as the next King of Israel. The cup is the cup of destiny. It is full because David knows what the LORD expects of him, and he knew what his future was to be.

You prepare a table for me even though my oppressors are near because you protect me; you had me anointed as your King with oil; my destiny has been foretold, and you will see that it happens.

Verse Six

David calls out to the Sefirah Chesed, knowing that Chesed's loving kindness will be with him all his days.

Indeed the Sefirah Chesed will bless me all the days of my life, and I will return into the house of the LORD for all time.

Complete Psalm Rewrite Emphasizing Spiritual Awareness

A psalm of David. It is the LORD who fed his people in the wilderness; they did not lack anything.

In my thirst, He will settle me in pleasant grass; he leads me to the peaceful waters to rest.

Again and again, He gives my flesh food, water, and rest; He also leads me in the paths of righteous justice for His Name's sake.

When I go into exile through the valley overshadowed by death, I fear no evil because You are with me; Your rod and Your staff comfort me.

You prepare a table for me even though my oppressors are near because you protect me; you had me anointed as your King with oil; my destiny has been foretold, and you will see that it happens.

Indeed the Sefirah Chesed will bless me all the days of my life, and I will return into the house of the LORD for all time.

Psalm 24

New American Standard 1995	Hebrew

Psa. 24:1   The *a*earth is the LORD'S, and [1]all it contains,

The *b*world, and those who dwell in it.

2   For He has *a*founded it upon the seas

And established it upon the rivers.

3   Who may *a*ascend into the *b*hill of the LORD?

And who may stand in His holy *c*place?

4   He who has *a*clean hands and a *b*pure heart,

Who has not *c*lifted up his soul [1]to falsehood

And has not *d*sworn deceitfully.

5   He shall receive a *a*blessing from the LORD

And [1]*b*righteousness from the God of his salvation.

6   [1]This is the generation of those who *a*seek Him,

Who seek Your face — *even* Jacob. [2]Selah.

Psa. 24:7   *a*Lift up your heads, O gates,

And be lifted up, O [1]ancient doors,

That the King of *b*glory may come in!

8   Who is the King of glory?

The LORD *a*strong and mighty,

The LORD *b*mighty in battle.

9   Lift up your heads, O gates,

And lift *them* up, O [1]ancient doors,

That the King of *a*glory may come in!

לְדָוִד מִזְמוֹר לַיהוָה הָאָרֶץ 1
וּמְלוֹאָהּ תֵּבֵל וְיֹשְׁבֵי בָהּ׃ 2 כִּי־
הוּא עַל־יַמִּים יְסָדָהּ וְעַל־
נְהָרוֹת יְכוֹנְנֶהָ׃ 3 מִי־יַעֲלֶה
בְהַר־יְהוָה וּמִי־יָקוּם בִּמְקוֹם
קָדְשׁוֹ׃ 4 נְקִי כַפַּיִם וּבַר־לֵבָב
אֲשֶׁר ׀ לֹא־נָשָׂא לַשָּׁוְא נַפְשִׁי
וְלֹא נִשְׁבַּע לְמִרְמָה׃ 5 יִשָּׂא
בְרָכָה מֵאֵת יְהוָה וּצְדָקָה
מֵאֱלֹהֵי יִשְׁעוֹ׃ 6 זֶה דּוֹר דֹּרְשׁוֹ
[דֹּרְשָׁיו] מְבַקְשֵׁי פָנֶיךָ יַעֲקֹב
סֶלָה׃ 7 שְׂאוּ שְׁעָרִים ׀ רָאשֵׁיכֶם
וְהִנָּשְׂאוּ פִּתְחֵי עוֹלָם וְיָבוֹא
מֶלֶךְ הַכָּבוֹד׃ 8 מִי זֶה מֶלֶךְ
הַכָּבוֹד יְהוָה עִזּוּז וְגִבּוֹר יְהוָה
גִּבּוֹר מִלְחָמָה׃ 9 שְׂאוּ שְׁעָרִים ׀
רָאשֵׁיכֶם וּשְׂאוּ פִּתְחֵי עוֹלָם
וְיָבֹא מֶלֶךְ הַכָּבוֹד׃ 10 מִי הוּא
זֶה מֶלֶךְ הַכָּבוֹד יְהוָה צְבָאוֹת
הוּא מֶלֶךְ הַכָּבוֹד סֶלָה׃ --

¹⁰ Who is this King of glory?
The LORD of ^ahosts,
He is the King of glory. Selah.

References

Psalm 24:1
[1]Lit *its fullness*
[a]1 Cor 10:26
[b]Ps 89:11

Psalm 24:2
[a]Ps 104:3, 5; 136:6

Psalm 24:3
[a]Ps 15:1
[b]Ps 2:6
[c]Ps 65:4

Psalm 24:4
[1]Or *in vain*
[a]Job 17:9; Ps 22:30; 26:6
[b]Ps 51:10; 73:1; Matt 5:8
[c]Ezek 18:15
[d]Ps 15:4

Psalm 24:5
[1]I.e. as vindicated
[a]Ps 115:13
[b]Ps 36:10

Psalm 24:6
[1]Or *Such*
[2]*Selah* may mean: *Pause, Crescendo* or *Musical interlude*
[a]Ps 27:4, 8

Psalm 24:7
[1]Lit *everlasting*
[a]Ps 118:20; Is 26:2
[b]Ps 29:2, 9; 97:6; Acts 7:2; 1 Cor 2:8

Psalm 24:8
[a]Deut 4:34; Ps 96:7
[b]Ex 15:3, 6; Ps 76:3-6

Psalm 24:9
[1]Lit *everlasting*
[a]Ps 26:8; 57:11

Psalm 24:10
[a]Gen 32:2; Josh 5:14; 2 Sam 5:10; Neh 9:6

Author's note: Selah is described by Rabbi Sampson Hirsch as instructing the reader to meditate on the statement/

Targum

Psa. 24:1 Of David. A Psalm. Behold, the earth and its creatures are the LORD's, the world and those who dwell in it. ² For he set a foundation on the seas and fixed it firmly on the rivers. ³ Who will ascend the mount of the LORD's sanctuary? And who will stand in his holy place? ⁴ One with clean hands and a pure mind, who has not sworn to a lie to make himself guilty, and who has not made an oath in guile. ⁵ He will receive blessings from the presence of the LORD, and generosity from God his redemption. ⁶ This is the generation that seeks him, that looks for his countenance, O Jacob, forever! ⁷ Lift up, O sanctuary gates, your heads; and stand erect, O eternal entrances, that the glorious king may enter. ⁸ Who is this glorious king? The LORD, strong and mighty, the LORD, a mighty ruler and one who wages battle. ⁹ Lift up your heads, O gates of the Garden of Eden; and stand erect, O eternal entrances, and the glorious king will enter. ¹⁰ Who is this glorious king? The LORD Sabaoth, he is the glorious king forever.

Spiritual Awareness

The spiritual rewrite for the verses are in bold.

Introduction

A goal for King David was to bring back the purity of Adam that existed before the Sin in the Garden of Eden. Ancient tradition says that Mount Moriah was the place where the LORD created Adam. Midrash Shocher Tov says that David purchased the land for the Temple from Aravna the Jebusite. David then erected a temporary altar upon which he offered sacrifices of thanksgiving (2 Samuel 24:18-25).

David intended the psalm to be recited on the day of the Temple's consecration. David believed that the presence of the LORD was in the world, and this psalm would concentrate the LORD to dwell upon the Ark of the Covenant. David was referring to the Shekinah.

Today this psalm is recited when the Torah scrolls are returned to the Ark during synagogue worship.

Verse one

הָאָרֶץ וּמְלוֹאָהּ (Ha-aretz vum'loa) – means "the earth and the fullness thereof." This is the fundamental prerequisite for all human life and development. The fullness of the Earth belongs to the LORD since the LORD created the Earth.

By David. A psalm. The earth is the LORD's and the fullness thereof. The world of men and all that dwell in it belong to the LORD.

Verse two

The LORD formed the world upon the seas and rivers for humankind. Nations developed because of the geography that the LORD created. Seas and rivers divided people into various nations. The LORD intended for the different climatic zones on the Earth by raising the lowering the altitude of the land. The LORD set history into motion because the world's nations would have different national characteristics and peculiarities.

The LORD formed the nations of the world upon the seas and rivers, which constantly guide history.

Verse three

The psalm reminds us that the ruling force or power on the Earth is the LORD through His Shekinah. The moral Law of Malkhut rules the Earth, not humans.

Who can ascend to the mountain of the LORD, and who can stand on Mount Moriah where the Temple is to be built?

Verse four

The "clean hands" is symbolic of an inner purity where everything impure has been removed. The possession of such a person is pure so that when touched, the person remains pure. Also, the possessions this person has were not obtained by any form of ill-gotten gains. The pure heart is a person who has a pure mind that harbors no impure thoughts.

This person also never uses words for the purpose of deception. Such a person will never swear falsely to deceive other persons.

He who obtained all possessions purely through clean hands and has only pure thoughts in his heart never used falsehoods and never swore an oath falsely.

Verse five

A person who always acts, thinks, and desires to conform to all the dictates of moral Law given by the LORD can expect to receive prosperity in whatever the person does in this world.

He will receive prosperity from the LORD and kindness from the God of his salvation.

Verse six

The generation living during David's tie sought after the LORD, thus, turning to Him for help and guidance. Every nation may retain its own characteristics and peculiarities. Still, each must live in conformity with the supreme divine moral Law. The reference to Jacob means "those that seek your face." This is because of the phrase מְבַקְשֵׁי פָנֶיךָ יַעֲקֹב (m'vach'shae panecha ya'kov). The expression is best translated as "the people of Jacob seek your countenance."

This is the generation that seeks after the LORD; the people of Jacob seek your countenance. Meditate on this verse.

Verse Seven

The order to open the gates is repeated. The first time human society did not heed the call to open the gates out of their own free will. Therefore, the author repeats this call by using an external force. The opening of the gates allows the King of Glory to come in.

Lift up your heads, o gates, and if not, let an external force open the doors that the King of Glory may enter.

Verse eight

The King of Glory is the LORD through His Shekinah. The Shekinah wants to be a part of human existence. The Shekinah is strong and invincible. The Shekinah is ready to battle any evil in this world.

Who is the King of Glory? The invincible and strong Shekinah will win every battle that She is involved in.

Verse nine

The author repeats his demand to open the gates. The future of the people is the portals – the gates.

Lift up your heads again, O gates, lift them up to become portals of the future so that the King of Glory (the Shekinah) may come in.

Verse ten

The author asks and answers the question as to who is the King of glory. The LORD is the King of glory. The Shekinah is His vehicle to feel his presence.

Who is the King of Glory? The LORD is the King of Glory. Meditate on this verse.

Complete Psalm Rewrite Emphasizing Spiritual Awareness

By David. A psalm. The earth is the LORD's and the fullness thereof. The world of men and all that dwell in it belong to the LORD.

The LORD formed the nations of the world upon the seas and rivers, which constantly guide history.

Who can ascend to the mountain of the LORD, and who can stand on Mount Moriah where the Temple is to be built?

He who obtained all possessions purely through clean hands and has only pure thoughts in his heart never used falsehoods and never swore an oath falsely.

He will receive prosperity from the LORD and kindness from the God of his salvation. This is the generation that seeks after the LORD; the people of Jacob seek your countenance. Meditate on this verse.

Lift up your heads, o gates, and if not, let an external force open the doors that the King of Glory may enter.

Who is the King of Glory? The invincible and strong Shekinah will win every battle that She is involved in.

Lift up your heads again, O gates, lift them up to become portals of the future so that the King of Glory (the Shekinah) may come in.

Who is the King of Glory? The LORD is the King of Glory. Meditate on this verse.

Psalm 25

New American Standard 1995	Hebrew
Psa. 25:0 *A Psalm* of David. **Psa. 25:1** To You, O LORD, I *a*lift up my soul. 2 O my God, in You *a*I trust, Do not let me *b*be ashamed; Do not let my *c*enemies exult over me. 3 Indeed, *a*none of those who wait for You will be ashamed; *1*Those who *b*deal treacherously without cause will be ashamed. **Psa. 25:4** *a*Make me know Your ways, O LORD; Teach me Your paths. 5 Lead me in *a*Your truth and teach me, For You are the *b*God of my salvation; For You I *c*wait all the day. 6 *a*Remember, O LORD, Your compassion and Your lovingkindnesses, For they have been *1b*from of old. 7 Do not remember the *a*sins of my youth or my transgressions; *b*According to Your lovingkindness remember me, For Your *c*goodness' sake, O LORD. **Psa. 25:8***a*Good and *b*upright is the LORD; Therefore He *c*instructs sinners in the way. 9 He *a*leads the *1*humble in justice, And He *b*teaches the *1*humble His way. 10 All the paths of the LORD are *a*lovingkindness and truth To *b*those who keep His covenant and His testimonies. 11 For *a*Your name's sake, O LORD, *b*Pardon my iniquity, for it is great.	Psa. 25:1 לְדָוִד אֵלֶיךָ יְהוָה נַפְשִׁי אֶשָּׂא: 2 אֱלֹהַי בְּךָ בָטַחְתִּי אַל־אֵבוֹשָׁה אַל־יַעַלְצוּ אֹיְבַי לִי: 3 גַּם כָּל־קוֶיךָ לֹא יֵבֹשׁוּ יֵבֹשׁוּ הַבּוֹגְדִים רֵיקָם: 4 דְּרָכֶיךָ יְהוָה הוֹדִיעֵנִי אֹרְחוֹתֶיךָ לַמְּדֵנִי: 5 הַדְרִיכֵנִי בַאֲמִתֶּךָ וְלַמְּדֵנִי כִּי־אַתָּה אֱלֹהֵי יִשְׁעִי אוֹתְךָ קִוִּיתִי כָּל־הַיּוֹם: 6 זְכֹר־רַחֲמֶיךָ יְהוָה וַחֲסָדֶיךָ כִּי מֵעוֹלָם הֵמָּה: 7 חַטֹּאות נְעוּרַי וּפְשָׁעַי אַל־תִּזְכֹּר כְּחַסְדְּךָ זְכָר־לִי־אַתָּה לְמַעַן טוּבְךָ יְהוָה: 8 טוֹב־וְיָשָׁר יְהוָה עַל־כֵּן יוֹרֶה חַטָּאִים בַּדָּרֶךְ: 9 יַדְרֵךְ עֲנָוִים בַּמִּשְׁפָּט וִילַמֵּד עֲנָוִים דַּרְכּוֹ: 10 כָּל־אָרְחוֹת יְהוָה חֶסֶד וֶאֱמֶת לְנֹצְרֵי בְרִיתוֹ וְעֵדֹתָיו: 11 לְמַעַן־שִׁמְךָ יְהוָה וְסָלַחְתָּ לַעֲוֹנִי כִּי רַב־הוּא: 12 מִי־זֶה הָאִישׁ יְרֵא יְהוָה יוֹרֶנּוּ בְּדֶרֶךְ יִבְחָר: 13 נַפְשׁוֹ בְּטוֹב תָּלִין וְזַרְעוֹ יִירַשׁ אָרֶץ: 14 סוֹד יְהוָה לִירֵאָיו וּבְרִיתוֹ לְהוֹדִיעָם: 15 עֵינַי תָּמִיד אֶל־יְהוָה כִּי הוּא־יוֹצִיא מֵרֶשֶׁת רַגְלָי: 16 פְּנֵה־אֵלַי וְחָנֵּנִי כִּי־יָחִיד וְעָנִי אָנִי: 17 צָרוֹת לְבָבִי הִרְחִיבוּ מִמְּצוּקוֹתַי הוֹצִיאֵנִי: 18 רְאֵה עָנְיִי וַעֲמָלִי וְשָׂא לְכָל־חַטֹּאותָי: 19 רְאֵה־אֹויְבַי כִּי־רָבּוּ וְשִׂנְאַת חָמָס שְׂנֵאוּנִי: 20 שָׁמְרָה נַפְשִׁי וְהַצִּילֵנִי אַל־אֵבוֹשׁ כִּי־חָסִיתִי בָךְ: 21 תֹּם־וָיֹשֶׁר יִצְּרוּנִי כִּי קִוִּיתִךָ: 22 פְּדֵה אֱלֹהִים אֶת־יִשְׂרָאֵל מִכֹּל צָרוֹתָיו: --

Psa. 25:12   Who is the man who *a*fears the LORD?
He will *b*instruct him in the way he should choose.
13 His soul will *a*abide in ¹prosperity, And his ²descendants will *b*inherit the ³land.
14 The ¹*a*secret of the LORD is for those who fear Him, ²And He will *b*make them know His covenant.
15   My *a*eyes are continually toward the LORD, For He will ¹*b*pluck my feet out of the net.

Psa. 25:16 *a*Turn to me and be gracious to me, For I am *b*lonely and afflicted.
17 ¹The *a*troubles of my heart are enlarged; Bring me *b*out of my distresses.
18 *a*Look upon my affliction and my ¹trouble, And *b*forgive all my sins.
19   Look upon my enemies, for they *a*are many, And they *b*hate me with violent hatred.
20 *a*Guard my soul and deliver me;
Do not let me *b*be ashamed, for I take refuge in You.
21 Let *a*integrity and uprightness preserve me, For *b*I wait for You.
22 *a*Redeem Israel, O God, Out of all his troubles.

References

Psalm 25:1
[a]Ps 86:4; 143:8

Psalm 25:2
[a]Ps 31:1
[b]Ps 25:20; 31:1
[c]Ps 13:4; 41:11

Psalm 25:3
[1]Or *Let those...be ashamed*
[a]Ps 37:9; 40:1; Is 49:23
[b]Ps 119:158; Is 21:2; Hab 1:13

Psalm 25:4
[a]Ex 33:13; Ps 27:11; 86:11

Psalm 25:5
[a]Ps 25:10; 43:3
[b]Ps 79:9
[c]Ps 40:1

Psalm 25:6
[1]Or *everlasting*
[a]Ps 98:3
[b]Ps 103:17

Psalm 25:7
[a]Job 13:26; 20:11
[b]Ps 51:1
[c]Ps 31:19

Psalm 25:8
[a]Ps 86:5

Psalm 25:9
[1]Or *afflicted*
[a]Ps 23:3
[b]Ps 27:11

Psalm 25:10
[a]Ps 40:11
[b]Ps 103:18

Psalm 25:11
[a]Ps 31:3; 79:9
[b]Ex 34:9

Psalm 25:12
[a]Ps 31:19
[b]Ps 25:8; 37:23

Psalm 25:13
[1]Lit *good*
[2]Lit *seed*
[3]Or *earth*
[a]Prov 1:33; Jer 23:6
[b]Ps 37:11; 69:36; Matt 5:5

Psalm 25:14
[1]Or *counsel* or *intimacy*
[2]Or *And His covenant, to make them know it*
[a]Prov 3:32; John 7:17
[b]Gen 17:1, 2

Psalm 25:15
[1]Lit *bring out*

^bPs 92:15
^cPs 32:8

Psalm 25:17
[1]Some commentators read *Relieve the troubles of my heart*
^aPs 40:12
^bPs 107:6

Psalm 25:18
[1]Lit *toil*
^a2 Sam 16:12; Ps 31:7
^bPs 103:3

Psalm 25:19
^aPs 3:1
^bPs 9:13

Psalm 25:20
^aPs 86:2
^bPs 25:2

Psalm 25:21
^aPs 41:12
^bPs 25:3

Psalm 25:22
^aPs 130:8

^aPs 123:2; 141:8
^bPs 31:4; 124:7

Psalm 25:16
^aPs 69:16
^bPs 143:4

Targum

Psa. 25:1 Of David. Before you, O LORD, I lift up my soul in prayer. ² O my God, in you I have put my trust; I will not be disappointed; my foes will not rejoice over me. ³ Truly, all who look to you will not be disappointed; robbers and rogues will be disappointed. ⁴ Show me your ways, O LORD; teach me your paths. ⁵ Lead me by your merit and teach me, for you are God, my redemption; in you I have placed my hope every day. ⁶ Remember your mercies, O LORD, and your favors, for they are eternal. ⁷ The sins of my youth and my transgressions do not remember; according to your goodness remember me, because of your grace, O LORD. ⁸ Good and upright is the LORD; therefore he teaches sinners on the path. ⁹ He guides the humble in judgment; and teaches the humble his way. ¹⁰ All the ways of the LORD are kindness and truth to those who keep his covenant and his testimony. ¹¹ Because of your Name, O LORD, you will forgive my sin, for it is great. ¹² Who is the man who is reverent in the presence of the LORD? He will teach him the way he has chosen. ¹³ His soul will lodge in kindness, and his children will inherit the earth. ¹⁴ The mystery of the LORD is revealed to those who fear him; and his covenant is to instruct them. ¹⁵ My eyes look always before the LORD, for he will bring my feet out of the trap. ¹⁶ Look towards me and have mercy on me, for I am alone and afflicted. ¹⁷ The troubles of my heart have spread; bring me out of my anguish. ¹⁸ See my pain and vexation, and forgive all my sins. ¹⁹ See my foes, for they have become many; and the enmity that the rapacious have towards me. ²⁰ Keep my soul and save me; I would not be disappointed because I hoped in you. ²¹ Innocence and honesty will guard me, for I hoped in your word. ²² Redeem Israel, O LORD, from all his troubles.

Spiritual Awareness

The spiritual rewrite for the verses is in bold. The NASB gives a good picture of the spiritual awareness in the Psalm with the commentary offered. Therefore, a rewrite is not necessary.

Introduction

This Psalm describes King David's lifelong struggle to be on the "Path of the Upright." He begs for the LORD's assistance to help him stay on this path. The Sage Radak noted that this is the first Psalm arranged in the Alph-Beis, which means the first letters of the respective verses are in alphabetical order. However, the bet, vuv and kaf, letters are missing. It is unknown why David wrote the Psalm in this manner and why he left out the three missing letters.

Superscript

The NASB 1995 says, "A Psalm of David." The actual Hebrew says "of David."

Verse one

Lifting up the soul means bringing it closer to the LORD. In the Tree of Life, it would mean moving up a rung on the Ladder of Ascent. If a soul was in Malkhut, it would move to Yesod. From Yesod to Hod and so on. Moving up the ladder brings the soul closer to Keter and eventually to Ein Sof. David wished his soul to move closer to the LORD, which allowed the LORD to have a stronger hold on his direction. The Targum adds the words "in prayer." It is through prayer that the soul can move closer to the LORD.

Verse two

David placed all his trust and faith in the LORD, who ruled his destiny and guided his acts. He asked the LORD to help him to be satisfied with whatever happened in his life. By saying that he will not be ashamed by the results, he acknowledges that he will not be disappointed.

Verse three

No one who waits for divine assistance will be disappointed. The people who deal treacherously are those who have lost patience with waiting for the LORD. It is not a person's place to determine when and how the LORD will react to prayer or any assistance. Patience is required when waiting for the proper time that the LORD will assist. A breach of faith is always in vain because the person will become grievously disappointed. After all, what the person seeks will not be found.

Verse four

David wanted to know what the LORD had in store for him. He wanted to be shown the paths that his life would take. Was David showing patience by praying for the paths before the LORD was willing to share them with Him? A person can pray for the LORD to reveal His path for their life. Just remember that it is in the LORD's time that certain things may happen.

Verse five

The LORD can teach people how to behave appropriately. This includes a relationship with the LORD. David strived to be closer in his relationship with the LORD.

Verse six

David is asking the LORD to take care of him in the same way his mother attended to him when he was an infant. David became an adult, his mother's love for him would have changed from protector to supporter. The LORD was with David in his youth, even before David knew Him, and now that he was an adult, he still needed the love of the LORD to support him.

Verse seven

David asks the LORD to forget his childhood and youth mistakes. Children transgress the LORD's Law because they are not yet familiar with the Laws. David asks for the LORD's forgiveness for the transgressions of his youth.

Verse eight

The LORD deals kindly with humans and wants the best for us. However, at the same time, He expects us to live in a way that is worthy of His favor. The LORD does not abandon anyone who sins habitually. The LORD can strengthen a morally weak person. Such a person only needs to ask the LORD in prayer for the moral strength not to sin before Him.

Verse nine

The humble are persons whom the LORD has disciplined through judgment, the Sefirah Gevurah. Sinners, beware that the LORD seeks you out to change you and prepare your soul to return to the Lower Waters of Heaven.

Verse ten

This verse is in parallel with verse nine. Even the judgment of Gevurah does not mean that the love of the LORD from Chesed is not available to the person. The LORD created His covenant through Abraham and will always strive to make that happen.

Verse Eleven

The Name of the LORD (YHVH) offers a better future and renewed life for all who call upon the Name. The Name of the LORD is not spoken, but one can visualize it on paper or in mind. The Tzuruf prayer method is to see the Name of the LORD in front of you. Then see your prayers as beams of light passing through the Name. The prayers are acceptable to the LORD pass through the Name and are sanctified. The prayers that are not passed on are absorbed by the letters of the Name.

Verse twelve & thirteen

This is the result of a person who holds the LORD in reverence. The NASB uses the word "fear." Humans do not need to fear the LORD. Instead, they need to show reverence. This means that humans are to follow the ways and Laws that the LORD has given us, which are found in His Torah. When that is done, prosperity comes in this life to the person and his/her descendants. Having a good life means passing on a wonderful life to children. The children mainly model their parents' behavior. For the children that do this, their lives will be filled with prosperity.

Verse fourteen

This verse is a parallel verse because this idea has already been presented. The LORD will make known His presence to all who show reverence to Him by following the Torah. The covenant from the LORD is always in place. However, the people who respect the LORD will feel the results of the His presence and security.

Verse fifteen

David knew that the LORD was to deliver him from the tribulations of his life. The behavior that would have ensnared him into sin had been removed from his life path.

Verse sixteen

This verse is a parallel because this idea has already been presented. David tells the LORD that without His aid that David has no way to go. David needed the LORD to direct his life path, and he repeats the need for it.

Verse seventeen

This verse is a parallel because this idea has already been presented. David asks the LORD to bring him out of the troubles that have arisen in his life.

Verse eighteen

This verse is a parallel because this idea has already been presented. David knew that he had sinned greatly and grievously. Therefore, he prayed that the LORD will forgive him for these sins.

Verse nineteen

David believed that his sins caused Gevurah to bring up enemies who were to disciple him. Unfortunately, that discipline was David's death. That was not the punishment that he was looking for.

Verse twenty

The measure of David's sins was so great that he called upon the LORD to guard him against any future sins.

Verse twenty-one

David was looking for moral perfection and honest uprightness in his relations with his fellow persons. The later part of the verse is the statement that David knew that the LORD would help him.

Verse twenty-two

When David placed this Psalm into Israel's national collection of hymns, he added this final verse. David asked the LORD to forgive the nation for all its transgressions against the Torah.

Psalm 26

New American Standard 1995	Hebrew
Psa. 26:0 *A Psalm* of David. **Psa. 26:1** [1][a]Vindicate me, O LORD, for I have [b]walked in my integrity, And I have [c]trusted in the LORD [2][d]without wavering. 2 [a]Examine me, O LORD, and try me; [b]Test my [1]mind and my heart. 3 For Your [a]lovingkindness is before my eyes, And I have [b]walked in Your [1]truth. 4 I do not [a]sit with [1]deceitful men, Nor will I go with [2][b]pretenders. 5 I [a]hate the assembly of evildoers, And I will not sit with the wicked. 6 I shall [a]wash my hands in innocence, And I will go about [b]Your altar, O LORD, 7 That I may proclaim with the voice of [a]thanksgiving And declare all Your [1]wonders. **Psa. 26:8** O LORD, I [a]love the habitation of Your house And the place [1]where Your [b]glory dwells. 9 [a]Do not [1]take my soul away *along* with sinners, Nor my life with [b]men of bloodshed, 10 In whose hands is a [a]wicked scheme, And whose right hand is full of [b]bribes.	Psa. 26:1 לְדָוִ֨ד ׀ שָׁפְטֵ֤נִי יְהֹוָ֗ה כִּי־אֲנִ֤י בְתֻמִּ֣י הָלַ֑כְתִּי וּבַיהֹוָ֥ה בָּ֝טַ֗חְתִּי לֹ֣א אֶמְעָ֑ד ׃ 2 בְּחָנֵ֣נִי יְהֹוָ֣ה וְנַסֵּ֑נִי צׇרׄפָה [צׇרְפָ֖ה] כִלְיוֹתַ֣י וְלִבִּֽי ׃ 3 כִּי־חַ֭סְדְּךָ לְנֶ֣גֶד עֵינָ֑י וְ֝הִתְהַלַּ֗כְתִּי בַּאֲמִתֶּֽךָ ׃ 4 לֹא־יָ֭שַׁבְתִּי עִם־מְתֵי־ שָׁ֑וְא וְעִ֥ם נַ֝עֲלָמִ֗ים לֹ֣א אָבֽוֹא ׃ 5 שָׂ֭נֵאתִי קְהַ֣ל מְרֵעִ֑ים וְעִם־רְ֝שָׁעִ֗ים לֹ֣א אֵשֵֽׁב ׃ 6 אֶרְחַ֣ץ בְּנִקָּי֣וֹן כַּפָּ֑י וַאֲסֹבְבָ֖ה אֶת־מִזְבַּחֲךָ֣ יְהֹוָֽה ׃ 7 לַ֭שְׁמִעַ בְּק֣וֹל תּוֹדָ֑ה וּ֝לְסַפֵּ֗ר כׇּל־ נִפְלְאוֹתֶֽיךָ ׃ 8 יְ֭הֹוָה אָהַ֣בְתִּי מְע֣וֹן בֵּיתֶ֑ךָ וּ֝מְק֗וֹם מִשְׁכַּ֥ן כְּבוֹדֶֽךָ ׃ 9 אַל־ תֶּאֱסֹ֣ף עִם־חַטָּאִ֣ים נַפְשִׁ֑י וְעִם־ אַנְשֵׁ֖י דָמִ֣ים חַיָּֽי ׃ 10 אֲשֶׁר־בִּידֵיהֶ֥ם זִמָּ֑ה וִ֝ימִינָ֗ם מָ֣לְאָה שֹּֽׁחַד ׃ 11 וַ֭אֲנִי בְּתֻמִּ֣י אֵלֵ֑ךְ פְּדֵ֥נִי וְחׇנֵּֽנִי ׃ 12 רַגְלִ֗י עָ֥מְדָ֥ה בְמִישׁ֑וֹר בְּ֝מַקְהֵלִ֗ים אֲבָרֵ֥ךְ יְהֹוָֽה ׃

11   But as for me, I shall [a]walk in my integrity;
    [b]Redeem me, and be gracious to me.
12   [a]My foot stands on a [b]level place;
    In the [c]congregations I shall bless the LORD.	

References

Psalm 26:1
[1]Lit *Judge*
[2]Lit *I do not slide*
[a]Ps 7:8
[b]2 Kin 20:3; Prov 20:7
[c]Ps 13:5; 28:7
[d]Heb 10:23

Psalm 26:2
[1]Lit *kidneys,* figurative for inner man
[a]Ps 17:3; 139:23
[b]Ps 7:9

Psalm 26:3
[1]Or *faithfulness*
[a]Ps 48:9
[b]2 Kin 20:3; Ps 86:11

Psalm 26:4
[1]Or *worthless men;* lit *men of falsehood*
[2]Or *dissemblers, hypocrites*
[a]Ps 1:1
[b]Ps 28:3

Psalm 26:5
[a]Ps 31:6; 139:21

Psalm 26:6
[a]Ps 73:13
[b]Ps 43:3, 4

Psalm 26:7
[1]Or *miracles*
[a]Ps 9:1

Psalm 26:8
[1]Lit *of the tabernacle of Your glory*
[a]Ps 27:4
[b]Ps 24:7

Psalm 26:9
[1]Lit *gather*
[a]Ps 28:3
[b]Ps 139:19

Psalm 26:10
[a]Ps 37:7
[b]Ps 15:5

Psalm 26:11
[a]Ps 26:1
[b]Ps 44:26; 69:18

Psalm 26:12
[a]Ps 40:2
[b]Ps 27:11
[c]Ps 22:22

Targum

Psa. 26:1 Of David. Judge me, O LORD, for I have walked in my innocence; and in the LORD I have hoped [and] trusted; I shall not be shaken. **2** Try me, O LORD, and prove me; purify my inmost thoughts. **3** Because your goodness is before my eyes, and I have walked in your truth. **4** I have not reclined [to dine] with lying men; and I will not enter with those who hide themselves to do evil. **5** I hate the gathering of evildoers, and with the wicked I will not recline [to dine]. **6** I will sanctify my hands by my merit, and I have gone around your altar, O LORD. **7** To make heard the sound of praise, and to tell of all your wonders. **8** O LORD, I love the dwelling of your sanctuary, and the place of your glorious tabernacle. **9** My soul will not gather with the sinners, nor my life with the men who shed blood. **10** In whose hands is the purpose of sinning; their right hands are full of bribes. **11** But I will go about in my innocence; redeem me and have mercy on me. **12** My foot stands upright; in the gathering of the righteous I will bless the LORD.

Spiritual Awareness

The spiritual rewrite for the verses is in bold.

Introduction

This Psalm contains various desires David's lifelong aspirations: perfect innocence, purity, clarity of vision, truth, separation from evil, cleanliness, and zeal. David strived to become worthy of building the LORD's Temple in Jerusalem.

Verse one

שָׁפְטֵנִי (shap'tawnee) – means "to judge." The NASB uses the translation of "vindicate." The Targum uses the translation of "judge," which is more accurate. David asked the LORD to judge his life's actions. He wanted to build the LORD's house in Jerusalem. David knew that he had to become as pure as possible. The request is for the LORD to judge his life and determine if he was worthy of such an honor.

Judge me, LORD, for I have walked in my integrity and have trusted in you without any doubt.

Verse two

David knew that he needed the aid of the LORD to attain his moral goals. Therefore, he implores the LORD to examine his soul to see if he is worthy of serving. In addition, David asks the LORD to test him to see whether he is capable of more.

Examine me, Lord, and put me to the test to see if I can achieve more.

Verse three

David recognized that the Sefirah Chesed was always with him. Chesed offers the lovingkindness of the LORD.

The power of Chesed was always with me, and I have walked in your truth.

Verse four

David said that he did not deal with people who had no conception of the deeper meaning of life because they were interested in the vanity of materialism. He also avoided dealing with people who did not believe in the LORD.

I do not sit with materialistic only men, nor with anyone who does not believe in you.

Verse five

David detested engaging with people who were evil or wicked.

I have hated every gathering of wicked persons and will not be seated with the lawless.

Verse six

Paths of divine truth are revealed and established in several ways. One prerequisite to divine truth is to not associate with people who can lead one astray from the LORD by their words or actions.

I washed my hands in purity when I wanted to step within the circle of Your altar LORD.

Verse seven

לִשְׁמִעַ (lash'meea) – means "to become loud." The construction of the word, which is missing two letters (yud and hey), denotes saying something that other persons can hear. One purpose of communal worship is to acknowledge our debt to the LORD in the presence of other people. *Lash'meea* implies that David spoke these words while in the presence of other people. He was expressing his gratitude to the LORD with other worshipers.

May the voice of thanksgiving be heard as it tells them about your wondrous works.

Verse eight

David wanted to build the Temple, and he expressed that desire.

LORD, I love the chance to build Your house where your Shekinah can dwell.

Verse nine and ten

David repeats his resolution to live such a life that his soul will not perish in sensual levity, nor will it be absorbed by crimes against his fellow-men.

Do not take away my soul with sinners, nor my life with men who commit bloodshed, who reach out with their hands of lust, and the right hand has bribes.

Verse eleven

David repeats verse one and repeats his request for redemption.

But as for me, I shall walk on my integrity, redeem me with your favor.

Verse twelve

David found firm footing when his goals of purity had been reached.

My foot now stands on the firm foundation of purity. I go to the congregation to bless the LORD.

Complete Psalm Rewrite Emphasizing Spiritual Awareness

Judge me, LORD, for I have walked in my integrity and have trusted in you without any doubt.

Examine me, Lord, and put me to the test to see if I can achieve more.

The power of Chesed was always with me, and I have walked in your truth.

I do not sit with materialistic only men, nor with anyone who does not believe in you.

I have hated every gathering of wicked persons and will not be seated with the lawless.

I washed my hands in purity when I wanted to step within the circle of Your altar LORD.

May the voice of thanksgiving be heard as it tells them about your wondrous works.

LORD, I love the chance to build Your house where your Shekinah can dwell.

Do not take away my soul with sinners, nor my life with men who commit bloodshed, who reach out with their hands of lust, and the right hand has bribes.

But as for me, I shall walk on my integrity, redeem me with your favor.

My foot now stands on the firm foundation of purity. I go to the congregation to bless the LORD.

New American Standard 1995	Hebrew

New American Standard 1995

Psa. 27:1   The LORD is my [a]light and my [b]salvation;

Whom shall I fear?

The LORD is the [1c]defense of my life;

[d]Whom shall I dread?

2   When evildoers came upon me to [a]devour my flesh,

My adversaries and my enemies, they [b]stumbled and fell.

3   Though a [a]host encamp against me,

My heart will not fear;

Though war arise against me,

In *spite of* this I [1]shall be [b]confident.

Psa. 27:4   [a]One thing I have asked from the LORD, that I shall seek:

That I may [b]dwell in the house of the LORD all the days of my life,

To behold [c]the [1]beauty of the LORD

And to [2d]meditate in His temple.

5   For in the [a]day of trouble He will [b]conceal me in His [1]tabernacle;

In the secret place of His tent He will [c]hide me;

He will [d]lift me up on a rock.

6   And now [a]my head will be lifted up above my enemies around me,

And I will offer in His tent [b]sacrifices [1]with shouts of joy;

I will [c]sing, yes, I will sing praises to the LORD.

Hebrew

לְדָוִד ׀ יְהֹוָה ׀ אוֹרִי Psa. 27:1
וְיִשְׁעִי מִמִּי אִירָא יְהֹוָה
מָעוֹז־חַיַּי מִמִּי אֶפְחָד׃ 2
בִּקְרֹב עָלַי ׀ מְרֵעִים לֶאֱכֹל
אֶת־בְּשָׂרִי צָרַי וְאֹיְבַי לִי
הֵמָּה כָשְׁלוּ וְנָפָלוּ׃ אִם־ 3
תַּחֲנֶה עָלַי ׀ מַחֲנֶה לֹא־יִירָא
לִבִּי אִם־תָּקוּם עָלַי מִלְחָמָה
בְּזֹאת אֲנִי בוֹטֵחַ׃ אַחַת ׀ 4
שָׁאַלְתִּי מֵאֵת־יְהֹוָה אוֹתָהּ
אֲבַקֵּשׁ שִׁבְתִּי בְּבֵית־יְהֹוָה
כָּל־יְמֵי חַיַּי לַחֲזוֹת בְּנֹעַם־
יְהֹוָה וּלְבַקֵּר בְּהֵיכָלוֹ׃ כִּי 5
יִצְפְּנֵנִי ׀ בְּסֻכֹּה בְּיוֹם רָעָה
יַסְתִּרֵנִי בְּסֵתֶר אָהֳלוֹ בְּצוּר
יְרוֹמְמֵנִי׃ וְעַתָּה יָרוּם 6
רֹאשִׁי עַל אֹיְבַי סְבִיבוֹתַי
וְאֶזְבְּחָה בְאָהֳלוֹ זִבְחֵי
תְרוּעָה אָשִׁירָה וַאֲזַמְּרָה
לַיהֹוָה׃ שְׁמַע־יְהֹוָה קוֹלִי 7

Psa. 27:7   *a*Hear, O LORD, when I cry with my voice,

And be gracious to me and *b*answer me.

8   *When You said*, "*a*Seek My face," my heart said to You,

"Your face, O LORD, *b*I shall seek."

9   *a*Do not hide Your face from me,

Do not turn Your servant away in *b*anger;

You have been *c*my help;

*d*Do not abandon me nor *e*forsake me,

O God of my salvation!

10   *1*For my father and *a*my mother have forsaken me,

But *b*the LORD will take me up.

Psa. 27:11   *a*Teach me Your way, O LORD,

And lead me in a *b*level path

Because of *1*my foes.

12   Do not deliver me over to the *1a*desire of my adversaries,

For *b*false witnesses have risen against me,

And such as *c*breathe out violence.

13   *1I would have despaired* unless I had believed that I would see the *a*goodness of the LORD

In the *b*land of the living.

14   *a*Wait for the LORD;

Be *b*strong and let your heart take courage;

Yes, wait for the LORD.

אֶקְרָא וְחָנֵּנִי וַעֲנֵנִי: לְךָ ׀ 8

אָמַר לִבִּי בַּקְּשׁוּ פָנָי אֶת־

פָּנֶיךָ יְהוָה אֲבַקֵּשׁ: אַל־ 9

תַּסְתֵּר פָּנֶיךָ ׀ מִמֶּנִּי אַל־

תַּט־בְּאַף עַבְדֶּךָ עֶזְרָתִי

הָיִיתָ אַל־תִּטְּשֵׁנִי וְאַל־

תַּעַזְבֵנִי אֱלֹהֵי יִשְׁעִי: כִּי־ 10

אָבִי וְאִמִּי עֲזָבוּנִי וַיהוָה

יַאַסְפֵנִי: הוֹרֵנִי יְהוָה 11

דַּרְכֶּךָ וּנְחֵנִי בְּאֹרַח מִישׁוֹר

לְמַעַן שׁוֹרְרָי: אַל־תִּתְּנֵנִי 12

בְּנֶפֶשׁ צָרָי כִּי קָמוּ־בִי עֵדֵי־

שֶׁקֶר וִיפֵחַ חָמָס: לוּלֵא 13

הֶאֱמַנְתִּי לִרְאוֹת בְּטוּב־יְהוָה

בְּאֶרֶץ חַיִּים: קַוֵּה אֶל־ 14

יְהוָה חֲזַק וְיַאֲמֵץ לִבֶּךָ וְקַוֵּה

אֶל־יְהוָה:

References

Psalm 27:1
[1]Or *refuge*
[a]Ps 18:28; Is 60:20; Mic 7:8
[b]Ex 15:2; Ps 62:7; 118:14; Is 33:2; Jon 2:9
[c]Ps 28:8
[d]Ps 118:6

Psalm 27:2
[a]Ps 14:4
[b]Ps 9:3

Psalm 27:3
[1]Lit *am confident*
[a]Ps 3:6
[b]Job 4:6

Psalm 27:4
[1]Lit *delightfulness*
[2]Lit *inquire*
[a]Ps 26:8
[b]Ps 23:6
[c]Ps 90:17
[d]Ps 18:6

Psalm 27:5
[1]Or *shelter*
[a]Ps 50:15
[b]Ps 31:20
[c]Ps 17:8
[d]Ps 40:2

Psalm 27:6
[1]Lit *of shouts*
[a]Ps 3:3
[b]Ps 107:22
[c]Ps 13:6

Psalm 27:7

Psalm 27:7
[a]Ps 4:3; 61:1
[b]Ps 13:3

Psalm 27:8
[a]Ps 105:4; Amos 5:6
[b]Ps 34:4

Psalm 27:9
[a]Ps 69:17
[b]Ps 6:1
[c]Ps 40:17
[d]Ps 94:14
[e]Ps 37:28

Psalm 27:10
[1]Or *If my father...forsake me, Then the LORD*
[a]Is 49:15
[b]Is 40:11

Psalm 27:11
[1]Or *those who lie in wait for me*
[a]Ps 25:4; 86:11
[b]Ps 5:8; 26:12

Psalm 27:12
[1]Lit *soul*
[a]Ps 41:2
[b]Deut 19:18; Ps 35:11; Matt 26:60
[c]Acts 9:1

Psalm 27:13
[1]Or *Surely I believed*
[a]Ps 31:19
[b]Job 28:13; Ps 52:5; 116:9; 142:5; Is 38:11; Jer 11:19; Ezek 26:20

^aPs 4:3; 61:1
^bPs 13:3

Psalm 27:8
^aPs 105:4; Amos 5:6
^bPs 34:4

Psalm 27:9
^aPs 69:17
^bPs 6:1
^cPs 40:17
^dPs 94:14
^ePs 37:28

Psalm 27:10
¹Or *If my father...forsake me, Then the LORD*
^aIs 49:15
^bIs 40:11

Psalm 27:11
¹Or *those who lie in wait for me*
^aPs 25:4; 86:11
^bPs 5:8; 26:12

Psalm 27:12
¹Lit *soul*
^aPs 41:2
^bDeut 19:18; Ps 35:11; Matt 26:60
^cActs 9:1

Psalm 27:13
¹Or *Surely I believed*
^aPs 31:19
^bJob 28:13; Ps 52:5; 116:9; 142:5; Is 38:11; Jer 11:19; Ezek 26:20

Psalm 27:14
^aPs 25:3; 37:34; 40:1; 62:5; 130:5; Prov 20:22; Is 25:9
^bPs 31:24

Targum

27:1 Of David. The LORD is my light and my redemption; whom shall I fear? The LORD is the strength of my life; whom shall I fear? [2] Whenever evildoers come near to me to destroy my flesh, my oppressors and my foes – they have stumbled and fallen. [3] If an army of the wicked encamps against me, my heart will not fear; if battle rises against me, in this I place my hope. [4] One thing I have sought from the presence of the LORD; that thing I will continue to seek: that I should dwell in the sanctuary of the LORD all the days of my life, to see the pleasantness of the LORD and to inquire in his temple. [5] For he will hide me in his shadow in the day of evil, he will conceal me in the hiding place of his tabernacle, in a mighty fortress he will raise me up. [6] And now my head will be lifted up over my enemies round about; and I will slaughter acceptable sacrifices in his tabernacle; I will sing praise and be glad in the presence of the LORD. [7] Receive, O LORD, my prayer when I call, and have mercy on me and pity me. [8] To you my heart said, "Seek my face"; your countenance, O LORD, I will seek. [9] Do not remove your presence from me; do not turn in anger to your servant; you have been my help; do not exile me and do not abandon me, O God my redemption. [10] Because my father (abba) and my mother have abandoned me, but the LORD will gather me in. [11] Teach me, O LORD, your ways, and lead me by a straight path because of my Psalm. [12] Do not hand me over to the will of my oppressors, for the false witnesses have risen against me, and those who speak rapacity. [13] Had I not believed I would look on the goodness of the LORD in the land of eternal life! [14] Hope in the LORD; strengthen and fortify your heart; and hope in the LORD. --

Spiritual Awareness

The spiritual rewrite would be so close to the current English translation that it was not done.

Introduction

This Psalm is used today during the "Days of Awe" in the month of Elul. It is recited on the festival of Succot by many Jews. The Psalm has nothing to do with repentance. However, it does teach us how to live without sin. A person who is fully engrossed in a single-minded dedication to the LORD has no room for sin. The Psalm expresses the thoughts and attitudes which filled David's spirit and guided him in his life on earth.

Verse one

David acknowledged that the LORD's greatness and might are so overwhelming that he felt tiny before him. David felt no fear because he knew that the LORD would not allow him to perish at the hands of men who did not believe in Him.

Verse two

רַע וְאֹיְבַי לִי (ra v'oy'va lee)- means "adversaries and enemies to." This phrase is a parenthetical expression meaning "I saw in them, my enemies." David saw certain persons as his enemy. However, the LORD views them as evildoers because they want to kill the LORD's anointed King.

Verse three

מַחֲנֶה (machaney) – means "enemy." This word is in the feminine gender in this sentence. Therefore, it shows that Davi deemed that this enemy that he spoke of could not harm him because he was stronger than them.

Verse four

To dwell in the house of the LORD all the days of my life does not mean that David wanted to spend every minute of his life in the Temple. Since the Temple in Jerusalem was not built yet, this phrase must have a different meaning. It describes the conception of life and the fulfillment of its duties set by the LORD, making any place a Divine sanctuary for the Shekinah. Any place can be transformed into a Temple for LORD.

Verse five

David knew that the LORD sheltered him from trouble. In this case, it was the enemies that he had. David took the throne of Israel by force. Samuel anointed him to become the King of Israel. However, when Saul and Jonathan died, other sons took the throne. A minor civil disturbance developed, and David and his army had to defeat the sons of Saul. Even when the fighting stopped, men loyal to Saul's house tried to remove David.

Verse six

While his enemies surrounded David, the LORD's presence was with him through his awareness of the Shekinah. He knew that he would survive any attack because the LORD anointed him to be the King of Israel. The LORD's Will must be followed. That helped David's concern of being murdered by Saul's followers.

Verse seven

This verse is interesting because since David expressed that he was sure that the LORD was with him, he still calls out for Divine grace to fall upon him. David asks for an answer to his calling, but he has it already. When looking at the remainder of the Psalm, David is asking for everything he just acknowledged that he had.

Verse eight

The LORD gave a Divine order to seek him. Humans cannot look upon the face of the LORD because death would occur. The LORD told Moses this when he was on Mount Sinai. Therefore, to search for the face of the LORD is to seek out the Shekinah so that the love and grace of the LORD can be felt.

Verse nine

David beseeches the LORD to make himself known to him.

Verse ten

Parental love is one of the most vital forms of love. For a child, only the love of the LORD is stronger. David knew that even if his parents stopped loving him that the LORD would never stop.

Verse eleven

David referred to his morality. He wanted to remain ethical in the face of enemies. In wartime, there are few rules. It is easy to break the laws of the LORD when faced with death. David wanted to remain as moral and ethical as possible during all times of crisis. David following the ways of the LORD was paramount to him.

Verse twelve

David did not want to become the person that his enemies wanted him to be. When a king was merciful and benevolent, the nobles of the kingdom would despise him. The nobles did not want to help the people. Instead, the nobles wanted to exploit the people. That cannot happen when the King is of high moral character. David refused to become a king that allowed the exploitation of his people by anyone.

Verse thirteen

David believed that if he survived his enemy's attacks, it was due to his faith in the LORD and his prayers. Faith pushed David to continue fighting for the LORD.

Verse fourteen

The conclusion to this Psalm is that we have to put our love and trust in the LORD. This verse is one of encouragement even if the results are not seen immediately.

New American Standard 1995	Hebrew

Psa. 28:1   To You, O LORD, I call;
My [a]rock, do not be deaf to me,
For if You [b]are silent to me,
I will become like those who [c]go down to the pit.
2   Hear the [a]voice of my supplications when I cry to You for help,
When I [b]lift up my hands [c]toward [1]Your holy [d]sanctuary.
3   [a]Do not drag me away with the wicked
And with those who work iniquity,
Who [b]speak peace with their neighbors,
While evil is in their hearts.
4   Requite them [a]according to their work and according to the evil of their practices;
Requite them according to the deeds of their hands;
Repay them their [1]recompense.
5   Because they [a]do not regard the works of the LORD
Nor the deeds of His hands,
He will tear them down and not build them up.

Psa. 28:6   Blessed be the LORD,
Because He [a]has heard the voice of my supplication.
7   The LORD is my [a]strength and my [b]shield;
My heart [c]trusts in Him, and I am helped;
Therefore [d]my heart exults,
And with [e]my song I shall thank Him.

הַפְּרוֹיֶקְט הָעִבְרִי

Psa. 28:1 לְדָוִד אֵלֶיךָ יְהוָה ׀ אֶקְרָא
צוּרִי אַל־תֶּחֱרַשׁ מִמֶּנִּי פֶּן־תֶּחֱשֶׁה
מִמֶּנִּי וְנִמְשַׁלְתִּי עִם־יוֹרְדֵי בוֹר׃ 2
שְׁמַע קוֹל תַּחֲנוּנַי בְּשַׁוְּעִי אֵלֶיךָ
בְּנָשְׂאִי יָדַי אֶל־דְּבִיר קָדְשֶׁךָ׃ 3
אַל־תִּמְשְׁכֵנִי עִם־רְשָׁעִים וְעִם־
פֹּעֲלֵי אָוֶן דֹּבְרֵי שָׁלוֹם עִם־רֵעֵיהֶם
וְרָעָה בִּלְבָבָם׃ 4 תֶּן־לָהֶם כְּפָעֳלָם
וּכְרֹעַ מַעַלְלֵיהֶם כְּמַעֲשֵׂה יְדֵיהֶם
תֵּן לָהֶם הָשֵׁב גְּמוּלָם לָהֶם׃ 5 כִּי
לֹא יָבִינוּ אֶל־פְּעֻלֹּת יְהוָה וְאֶל־
מַעֲשֵׂה יָדָיו יֶהֶרְסֵם וְלֹא יִבְנֵם׃ 6
בָּרוּךְ יְהוָה כִּי־שָׁמַע קוֹל תַּחֲנוּנָי׃
7 יְהוָה ׀ עֻזִּי וּמָגִנִּי בּוֹ בָטַח לִבִּי
וְנֶעֱזָרְתִּי וַיַּעֲלֹז לִבִּי וּמִשִּׁירִי
אֲהוֹדֶנּוּ׃ 8 יְהוָה עֹז־לָמוֹ וּמָעוֹז
יְשׁוּעוֹת מְשִׁיחוֹ הוּא׃ 9 הוֹשִׁיעָה ׀
אֶת־עַמֶּךָ וּבָרֵךְ אֶת־נַחֲלָתֶךָ וּרְעֵם
וְנַשְּׂאֵם עַד־הָעוֹלָם׃

8 The LORD is [1]their [a]strength, And He is a [2b]saving defense to His anointed. 9 [a]Save Your people and bless [b]Your inheritance; Be their [c]shepherd also, and [d]carry them forever.	

References

Psalm 28:1
*a*Ps 18:2
*b*Ps 35:22; 39:12; 83:1
*c*Ps 88:4; 143:7; Prov 1:12

Psalm 28:2
[1]Lit *the innermost place of Your sanctuary*
*a*Ps 140:6
*b*Ps 134:2; 141:2; Lam 2:19; 1 Tim 2:8
*c*Ps 5:7; 138:2
*d*1 Kin 6:5

Psalm 28:3
*a*Ps 26:9
*b*Ps 12:2; 55:21; 62:4; Jer 9:8

Psalm 28:4
[1]Or *dealings*
*a*Ps 62:12; 2 Tim 4:14; Rev 18:6; 22:12

Psalm 28:5
*a*Is 5:12

Psalm 28:6
*a*Ps 28:2

Psalm 28:7
*a*Ps 18:2; 59:17
*b*Ps 3:3
*c*Ps 13:5; 112:7
*d*Ps 16:9
*e*Ps 40:3; 69:30

Psalm 28:8
[1]A few mss and ancient versions read *the strength of His people*
[2]Or *refuge of salvation*
*a*Ps 20:6; 89:17
*b*Ps 27:1; 140:7

Psalm 28:9
*a*Ps 106:47
*b*Deut 9:29; 32:9; 1 Kin 8:51; Ps 33:12; 106:40
*c*Ps 80:1
*d*Deut 1:31; Is 40:11; 46:3; 63:9

Targum

Psa. 28:1 Of David. To you, O LORD, I cry; O my strength, do not be silent to me, lest, when you are silent, I become like those who descend to the pit. [2] Accept the voice of my petition when I pray to you, whenever I spread my hands in prayer before your temple. [3] Do not drag me away with the wicked or with those who do wrong; who speak peace with their fellows, while evil is in their hearts. [4] Give to them according to their deeds, and according to their evil deeds; according to the works of their hands, repay them; turn upon them their retribution. [5] Because they do not understand the Torah of the LORD or the works of his hands; he will tear them down and not rebuild them. [6] Blessed is the LORD because he has accepted the voice of my prayer. [7] The LORD is my strength and shield; on him my heart has set its hope; and you have aided me, and my heart exults; I will give thanks in his presence by my psalm. [8] The LORD is their strength and might; he is the redemption of his anointed. [9] Redeem your people and bless your inheritance; feed them and support them forever.

Spiritual Awareness

The spiritual rewrite for the verses is in bold.

Introduction

This psalm is similar to Psalm 27. In this Psalm, King David asked the LORD to release him from his temporal responsibilities so that he could devote himself to the LORD's service. This action would also allow him to repent for his past sins and bring him closer to the LORD.

Verse one

The LORD being silent, thus not communicating with David, means that the LORD remained distant from him. David desired to get closer and closer to the LORD. Even though he offered prayers, the LORD was not answering him. The souls that go down to the pit are in Sheol, where they are entirely cut off from any communication from the LORD.

To You, O LORD, do I call; My rock is not distant from me, for your silence makes me think you are not concerned with me. It is as if I died and you placed me in Sheol.

Verse two

David expected the LORD to help him because David had given his full devotion to the LORD's Law at this stage of his life.

Hear my supplications when I turn to You for help, when I lift up my hands toward your holy sanctuary.

Verse three

David said that he wants to seek out a future that only follows the path of the Law of the LORD.

Take me away from the lawless and the workers of violence, they speak peace with their neighbors, but evil is in their hearts.

Verse four

פָּעַל (paal) – means "to do." This word denotes attaining mastery over materials or circumstances as to be able to shape them following one's intentions. Therefore if one's intentions are evil, then their actions will be evil.

Give them according to their deed and according to the evil of their deeds; give them according to the work of their hands, let them be in their deserts, thus cut off from Your love and grace.

Verse five

Evil people have no respect for the LORD. Their actions are that of Satanic influence.

They give no heed to your works, nor the deeds of the LORD's hands; the LORD will tear them down and not build them up.

Verse six & seven

David felt that his prayers had already been heard because he understood the attitudes held by his foes toward the LORD and the Torah. These attitudes are quite different from those which he has always cherished.

Blessed be the LORD, for He has already heard the voice of my supplications.

The LORD is my strength and shield; my heart has trusted in Him, and I received His help; I rejoice and sing songs of praise to Him.

Verse eight

David knew that the LORD was an invincible force, and His power gave salvation to him.

The LORD is an invincible power to them and offers salvation to His anointed.

Verse nine

David knew that the LORD must be trusted. He prayed that His people would come to know Him as their leader (shepherd) forever.

Grant salvation to your people, who are your inheritance, and be their spiritual leader forever.

Complete Psalm Rewrite Emphasizing Spiritual Awareness

To You, O LORD, do I call; My rock is not distant from me, for your silence makes me think you are not concerned with me. It is as if I died and you placed me in Sheol.

Hear my supplications when I turn to You for help, when I lift up my hands toward your holy sanctuary.

Take me away from the lawless and the workers of violence, they speak peace with their neighbors, but evil is in their hearts.

Give them according to their deed and according to the evil of their deeds; give them according to the work of their hands, let them be in their deserts, thus cut off from Your love and grace.

They give no heed to your works, nor the deeds of the LORD's hands; the LORD will tear them down and not build them up.

Blessed be the LORD, for He has already heard the voice of my supplications.

The LORD is my strength and shield; my heart has trusted in Him, and I received His help; I rejoice and sing songs of praise to Him.

The LORD is an invincible power to them and offers salvation to His anointed.

Grant salvation to your people, who are your inheritance, and be their spiritual leader forever.

Psalm 29

New American Standard 1995	Hebrew
Psa. 29:0 A Psalm of David. **Psa. 29:1** [a]Ascribe to the LORD, O [1]sons of the mighty, Ascribe to the LORD glory and strength. [2] Ascribe to the LORD the glory [1]due to His name; Worship the LORD [a]in [2]holy array. **Psa. 29:3** The [a]voice of the LORD is upon the waters; The God of glory [b]thunders, The LORD is over [1c]many waters. [4] The voice of the LORD is [a]powerful, The voice of the LORD is majestic. [5] The voice of the LORD breaks the cedars; Yes, the LORD breaks in pieces [a]the cedars of Lebanon. [6] He makes Lebanon [a]skip like a calf, And [b]Sirion like a young wild ox. [7] The voice of the LORD hews out [1]flames of fire. [8] The voice of the LORD [1]shakes the wilderness; The LORD shakes the wilderness of [a]Kadesh. [9] The voice of the LORD makes [a]the deer to calve And strips the forests bare; And [b]in His temple everything says, "Glory!"	**Psa. 29:1** מִזְמוֹר לְדָוִד הָבוּ לַיהוָה בְּנֵי אֵלִים הָבוּ לַיהוָה כָּבוֹד וָעֹז׃ 2 הָבוּ לַיהוָה כְּבוֹד שְׁמוֹ הִשְׁתַּחֲווּ לַיהוָה בְּהַדְרַת־קֹדֶשׁ׃ 3 קוֹל יְהוָה עַל־הַמָּיִם אֵל־הַכָּבוֹד הִרְעִים יְהוָה עַל־מַיִם רַבִּים׃ 4 קוֹל־יְהוָה בַּכֹּחַ קוֹל יְהוָה בֶּהָדָר׃ 5 קוֹל יְהוָה שֹׁבֵר אֲרָזִים וַיְשַׁבֵּר יְהוָה אֶת־אַרְזֵי הַלְּבָנוֹן׃ 6 וַיַּרְקִידֵם כְּמוֹ־עֵגֶל לְבָנוֹן וְשִׂרְיֹן כְּמוֹ בֶן־רְאֵמִים׃ 7 קוֹל־יְהוָה חֹצֵב לַהֲבוֹת אֵשׁ׃ 8 קוֹל יְהוָה יָחִיל מִדְבָּר יָחִיל יְהוָה מִדְבַּר קָדֵשׁ׃ 9 קוֹל יְהוָה יְחוֹלֵל אַיָּלוֹת וַיֶּחֱשֹׂף יְעָרוֹת וּבְהֵיכָלוֹ כֻּלּוֹ אֹמֵר כָּבוֹד׃ 10 יְהוָה לַמַּבּוּל יָשָׁב וַיֵּשֶׁב יְהוָה מֶלֶךְ לְעוֹלָם׃ 11 יְהוָה עֹז לְעַמּוֹ יִתֵּן יְהוָה יְבָרֵךְ אֶת־עַמּוֹ בַשָּׁלוֹם׃

<table>
<tr><td>

Psa. 29:10   The LORD sat *as King* at the [a]flood;

    Yes, the LORD sits as [b]King forever.

11   [1]The LORD will give [a]strength to His people;

    [2]The LORD will bless His people with [b]peace.

</td><td></td></tr>
</table>

References

Psalm 29:1
[1]Or *sons of gods*
[a]1 Chr 16:28, 29; Ps 96:7-9

Psalm 29:2
[1]Lit *of His name*
[2]Or *the majesty of holiness*
[a]2 Chr 20:21; Ps 110:3

Psalm 29:3
[1]Or *great*
[a]Ps 104:7
[b]Job 37:4, 5; Ps 18:13
[c]Ps 18:16; 107:23

Psalm 29:4
[a]Ps 68:33

Psalm 29:5
[a]Judg 9:15; 1 Kin 5:6; Ps 104:16; Is 2:13; 14:8

Psalm 29:6
[a]Ps 114:4, 6
[b]Deut 3:9

Psalm 29:7
[1]I.e. lightning

Psalm 29:8
[1]Or *causes...to whirl*
[a]Num 13:26

Psalm 29:9
[a]Job 39:1
[b]Ps 26:8

Psalm 29:10
[a]Gen 6:17
[b]Ps 10:16

Psalm 29:11
[1]Or *May the LORD give*
[2]Or *May the LORD bless*
[a]Ps 28:8; 68:35; Is 40:29
[b]Ps 37:11; 72:3

Targum

Psa. 29:1 A psalm of David. Give praise in the presence of the LORD, O bands of angels; give glory and might in the LORD's presence. [2] Give the glory of his name in the presence of the LORD; bow down before the LORD in the splendor of holiness. [3] The voice of the LORD is heard above the waters; in his glorious might the LORD called out over many waters. [4] The voice of the LORD is heard in strength; the voice of the LORD is heard in splendor. [5] The voice of the LORD shatters cedars; the word of the LORD has shattered the cedars of Lebanon. [6] And he made them jump like a calf – Lebanon, and the Mount of Noisome Fruit, like the young of oxen. [7] The voice of the LORD splits flames of fire. [8] The voice of the LORD shakes the wilderness; the word of the LORD shakes the wilderness of Rekem. [9] The voice of the LORD impregnates the hinds, and makes the beasts of the forest give birth; and in his sanctuary above, all his servants say, "Glory," in his presence. [10] In the generation of the Flood, the LORD sat on his throne of judgment to take vengeance on them; and the LORD sat on the throne of mercy and saved Noah; and he reigns over his children forever and ever. [11] The LORD gave the Torah to his people; the LORD will bless his people in peace.

Spiritual Awareness

The spiritual rewrite for the verses is in bold.

Introduction

David wrote this Psalm in a continuation of Psalm 28. David vows to follow the LORD's Word. He was thankful for everything the LORD gave Him. This Psalm's purpose is to awaken our feelings of devoted obedience to the LORD.

Verse One

בְּנֵי אֵלִים (b'nay Elohim) – means "sons of God." This may have been a call to the people that those who are strong must remember that the LORD gives that gift. As humans, we are "sons of God" and not "God." It reminds us to be humble, especially before the LORD.

הָבוּ לַיהוָה כָּבוֹד (havu laAdonai c'dod) – means "ascribe to the LORD glory." Everything within you, your most incredible triumphs, comes from the LORD, and this must always be remembered. Without the LORD, each of us is nothing and would not exist.

A Psalm of David. Ascribe to the LORD all who are endowed with strength, ascribe to the LORD glory and might.

Verse two

The LORD's name must be honored above all names. It was believed that it was through the tetragrammaton that all powers from the LORD were made available to humans.

Ascribe to the LORD the glory due to his name, cast yourself down before the LORD in holiness's beauty.

Verse three

From this point on, the psalmist elaborates on the various manifestations of the LORD's revelation. The psalmist calls this revelation "the voice of the LORD."

The voice of the LORD is on the waters; God of glory thunders; the LORD is heard upon the surging waters.

Verse four

The voice of the LORD can be heard through His Law (the Torah). The LORD charges you to develop all moral potentialities. He also expects us to perfect our talents and faculties.

The voice of the LORD is within every force; His voice is in all beautiful things.

Verse 5, 6, & 7

The voice of the LORD can break through anything.

The voice of the LORD also breaks cedars, even as the LORD broke the cedars of Lebanon.

He makes them skip like calves, Lebanon and Sirion like an ox.

The voice of the LORD also blows out flames of fire.

Verse 8

This verse was a reminder of the events at Mount Sinai when the LORD spoke to the children of Israel.

The voice of the LORD shakes the wilderness; He also shakes the wilderness of Kadesh.

Verse 9

The voice of the LORD has tremendous power to affect what is happening on Earth.

The voice of the LORD makes deer calve, even while it strips the forests bare, and in His Temple, all that is His says "glory."

Verse 10

The LORD sat at the Flood can refer to anytime the LORD sits in judgment and sentences the Earth to some punishment. We need to remember that the LORD is watching the evil and sin in the world.

The LORD sat enthroned at the Flood. The LORD sits as King forever, always watching what we are doing.

Verse 11

The LORD gives strength to his people so that they can continue to praise Him. He also offers to His people peace and tranquility.

To His people, God will grant power to be victorious over all; the LORD will bless His people with peace.

Complete Psalm Rewrite Emphasizing Spiritual Awareness

A Psalm of David. Ascribe to the LORD all who are endowed with strength, ascribe to the LORD glory and might.

Ascribe to the LORD the glory due to his name, cast yourself down before the LORD in holiness's beauty.

The voice of the LORD is on the waters; God of glory thunders; the LORD is heard upon the surging waters.

The voice of the LORD is within every force; His voice is in all beautiful things.

The voice of the LORD also breaks cedars, even as the LORD broke the cedars of Lebanon.

He makes them skip like calves, Lebanon and Sirion like an ox.

The voice of the LORD also blows out flames of fire.

The voice of the LORD shakes the wilderness; He also shakes the wilderness of Kadesh.

The voice of the LORD makes deer calve, even while it strips the forests bare, and in His Temple, all that is His says "glory."

The LORD sat enthroned at the Flood. The LORD sits as King forever, always watching what we are doing.

To His people, God will grant power to be victorious over all; the LORD will bless His people with peace.

Psalm 30

New American Standard 1995	Hebrew
Psa. 30:0 A Psalm; a Song at the Dedication of the House. *A Psalm* of David. **Psa. 30:1** I will *a*extol You, O LORD, for You have *b*lifted me up, And have not let my *c*enemies rejoice over me. 2 O LORD my God, I *a*cried to You for help, and You *b*healed me. 3 O LORD, You have *a*brought up my soul from [1]Sheol; You have kept me alive, [2]that I would not *b*go down to the pit. 4 *a*Sing praise to the LORD, you *b*His godly ones, And *c*give thanks to His holy [1][d]name. 5 For *a*His anger is but for a moment, His *b*favor is for a lifetime; Weeping may [c]last for the night, But a shout of joy *comes* in the morning. **Psa. 30:6** Now as for me, I said in my prosperity, "I will *a*never be moved." 7 O LORD, by Your favor You have made my mountain to stand strong; You *a*hid Your face, I was dismayed. 8 To You, O LORD, I called,	1 מִזְמֹור שִׁיר־חֲנֻכַּת הַבַּיִת לְדָוִד׃ 2 אֲרֹומִמְךָ יְהוָה כִּי דִלִּיתָנִי וְלֹא־שִׂמַּחְתָּ אֹיְבַי לִי׃ 3 יְהוָה אֱלֹהָי שִׁוַּעְתִּי אֵלֶיךָ וַתִּרְפָּאֵנִי׃ 4 יְהוָה הֶעֱלִיתָ מִן־שְׁאֹול נַפְשִׁי חִיִּיתַנִי מִיֹּורְדִי־[מִ][יָרְדִי]־בֹור׃ 5 זַמְּרוּ לַיהוָה חֲסִידָיו וְהֹודוּ לְזֵכֶר קָדְשֹׁו׃ 6 כִּי רֶגַע בְּאַפֹּו חַיִּים בִּרְצֹונֹו בָּעֶרֶב יָלִין בֶּכִי וְלַבֹּקֶר רִנָּה׃ 7 וַאֲנִי אָמַרְתִּי בְשַׁלְוִי בַּל־אֶמֹּוט לְעֹולָם׃ 8 יְהוָה בִּרְצֹונְךָ הֶעֱמַדְתָּה לְהַרְרִי עֹז הִסְתַּרְתָּ פָנֶיךָ הָיִיתִי נִבְהָל׃ 9 אֵלֶיךָ יְהוָה אֶקְרָא וְאֶל־אֲדֹנָי אֶתְחַנָּן׃ 10 מַה־ בֶּצַע בְּדָמִי בְּרִדְתִּי אֶל־שָׁחַת הֲיֹודְךָ עָפָר הֲיַגִּיד אֲמִתֶּךָ׃ 11 שְׁמַע־יְהוָה וְחָנֵּנִי יְהוָה הֱיֵה־עֹזֵר לִי׃ 12 הָפַכְתָּ מִסְפְּדִי לְמָחֹול לִי פִּתַּחְתָּ שַׂקִּי וַתְּאַזְּרֵנִי שִׂמְחָה׃ 13 לְמַעַן יְזַמֶּרְךָ כָבֹוד וְלֹא יִדֹּם יְהוָה אֱלֹהַי לְעֹולָם אֹודֶךָּ׃

And to the Lord I made supplication:

9 "What profit is there in my blood, if I *a*go down to the pit?

Will the *b*dust praise You? Will it declare Your faithfulness?

Psa. 30:10 "*a*Hear, O LORD, and be gracious to me;

O LORD, be my *b*helper."

11 You have turned for me *a*my mourning into dancing;

You have *b*loosed my sackcloth and girded me with *c*gladness,

12 That *my* *1a*soul may sing praise to You and not be silent.

O LORD my God, I will *b*give thanks to You forever.

References

<table>
<tr><td valign="top" width="50%">

Psalm 30:1
[a]Ps 118:28; 145:1
[b]Ps 3:3
[c]Ps 25:2; 35:19, 24

Psalm 30:2
[a]Ps 88:13
[b]Ps 6:2; 103:3; Is 53:5

Psalm 30:3
[1]I.e. the nether world
[2]Some mss read *from among those who go down*
[a]Ps 86:13
[b]Ps 28:1

Psalm 30:4
[1]Lit *memorial*
[a]Ps 149:1
[b]Ps 50:5
[c]Ps 97:12
[d]Ex 3:15; Ps 135:13; Hos 12:5

Psalm 30:5
[a]Ps 103:9; Is 26:20; 54:7, 8
[b]Ps 118:1
[c]Ps 126:5; 2 Cor 4:17

Psalm 30:6
[a]Ps 10:6; 62:2, 6

Psalm 30:7
[a]Deut 31:17; Ps 104:29; 143:7

Psalm 30:9
[a]Ps 28:1
[b]Ps 6:5

</td><td valign="top" width="50%">

Psalm 30:10
[a]Ps 4:1; 27:7
[b]Ps 27:9; 54:4

Psalm 30:11
[a]Eccl 3:4; Jer 31:4, 13
[b]Is 20:2
[c]Ps 4:7

Psalm 30:12
[1]Lit *glory*
[a]Ps 16:9; 57:8; 108:1
[b]Ps 44:8

</td></tr>
</table>

Targum

Psa. 30:1 A praise song for the dedication of the sanctuary. Of David. [2] I will praise you, O LORD, for you made me stand erect, and did not let my enemies rejoice over me. [3] O LORD my God, I prayed in your presence and you healed me. [4] O LORD, you raised my soul out of Sheol; you preserved me from going down to the pit. [5] Sing praise in the LORD's presence, you his devotees; and give thanks at the invocation of his holy one. [6] For his anger is but a moment; eternal life is his good pleasure. In the evening one goes to bed in tears, but in the morning one rises in praise. [7] And I said when I dwelt in trust, I will never be shaken. [8] O LORD, by your will you prepared the mighty mountains; you removed your presence, I became afraid. [9] In your presence, O LORD, I will cry out; and to you, O my God, I will pray. [10] <And I said,> What profit is there in my blood, when I descend to the grave? Can those who descend to the dust praise you? Will they tell of your faithfulness? [11] Accept, O LORD, my prayer, and have mercy on me; O LORD, be my helper. [12] You turned my lament into my celebration; you loosened my sackcloth and girded me with joy. [13] Because the nobles of the world will give you praise and not be silent, O LORD my God, I [too] will give you praise.

Spiritual Awareness

The spiritual rewrite for the verses is in bold.

Introduction

This Psalm was written for the dedication of Solomon's Temple in Jerusalem. It is reserved today for occasions of innovation. It is also used for the inauguration of a time of daily prayers of praise. The Psalm does not say one word about the Temple. It does seem odd that this Psalm was about the consecration of the Temple to the LORD when it never mentions it. Instead, this Psalm consists of a lifetime of experiences attesting to healing, deliverance, trials, and bliss.

Superscript

The superscript for this Psalm is verse one in Hebrew and Targum. It is called a Psalm of David even though it was written for the dedication of the House of the LORD. It was David who gave his son Solomon the instructions and directions to build and furnish the Temple. David also collected the materials that Solomon needed for the project.

A Psalm, a song of the dedication of the Temple, by David

Verse One

דִלִּיתָנִי (deeleetanee) – means "lifted." This word's meaning is derived from the word

דָּלָה (dala). This word means to draw water. The spiritual awareness of this word is to lift an object from the depths towards oneself and keep the object hanging suspended over that depth. The inference is that *deeleetanee* accurately describes the uniqueness of

David's position. Any person who relies entirely upon the LORD's guidance and direction is drawn up like water by the LORD. People whom the LORD do not draw up rely on some prop on earth below their feet. David's support was not from below but rather from above, that is, from the LORD. There is nothing on earth that can uphold or support us.

David's enemies tried to cast him into the depths of despair where he could have died. The LORD lifted him up above his enemies, and David was triumphant.

I extol You, LORD, for you have raised me from the depths and have not allowed my enemies to rejoice by their attempts to pull me into the depths.

Verse two and three

There was a point in David's life that he felt that he was being taken into Sheol (the grave), and the LORD raised him back to health.

O LORD, my God, I cried out to you, and you healed me.

O LORD, you brought my soul up from the grave; You kept me alive, that I would not go into the tomb.

Verse four

The demonstrations of the LORD's greatness led to the House of the LORD in Jerusalem. It represented a charge to all people to give of themselves to the LORD with complete devotion of self.

חֲסִידָיו (chaseedan) – means "holy one, saint." The Temple calls all saints of the LORD to draw near with thoughts and emotions of joyous exaltation. The scene at the Temple was one of serenity and joy.

All saints sing to the LORD and thanks to His holy Name.

Verse five

The ways of the LORD are nothing but gifts of life and joy.

For the LORD's anger is but for a moment, weeping will tarry for the night, and joy will come in the morning.

Verse six to eleven

These verses describe a serious moment in David's difficult life. It was an incident that eventually was resolved with gladness. It was a blissful gift of providence. The suffering that David experienced convinced him to stay with the LORD. That meant that he placed his hopes and trust in the LORD. He received the LORD's help then and throughout his entire life.

Now, as for me, I said in my prosperity, "I will never be moved."
O LORD, by Your favor, You have made my mountain to stand firm;
You hid Your face, I was dismayed.
To You, O LORD, I called, And to the Lord I made supplication:
"What profit is there in my blood if I go down to the pit? Will the dust praise You? Will it declare Your faithfulness? "Hear, O LORD, and be gracious to me; O LORD, be my helper."

You have turned for me my mourning into dancing; You have loosed my sackcloth and girded me with gladness.

Verse twelve

Everything we see and touch is a product of the LORD's greatness. It is the mighty force of the LORD that creates and sustains everything.

כָּבוֹד (kavod) – means "glorious or glory." The NASB translates this word as "soul." The psalmist was not just talking about his soul singing praises to the LORD but rather everything on earth singing. This singing is an acknowledgment by all of creation that the LORD reigns.

Therefore all that is glorious will sing to You, O LORD, I will give you thanks forever.

Complete Psalm Rewrite Emphasizing Spiritual Awareness

A Psalm, a song of the dedication of the Temple, by David

I extol You, LORD, for you have raised me from the depths and have not allowed my enemies to rejoice by their attempts to pull me into the depths.

O LORD, my God, I cried out to you, and you healed me.

O LORD, you brought my soul up from the grave; You kept me alive, that I would not go into the tomb.

All saints sing to the LORD and thanks to His holy Name.

For the LORD's anger is but for a moment, weeping will tarry for the night, and joy will come in the morning.

Now, as for me, I said in my prosperity, "I will never be moved."

O LORD, by Your favor, You have made my mountain to stand firm; You hid Your face, I was dismayed.

To You, O LORD, I called, And to the Lord I made supplication:

"What profit is there in my blood if I go down to the pit? Will the dust praise You? Will it declare Your faithfulness? "Hear, O LORD, and be gracious to me; O LORD, be my helper."

You have turned for me my mourning into dancing; You have loosed my sackcloth and girded me with gladness.

Therefore all that is glorious will sing to You, O LORD, I will give you thanks forever.

Appendix

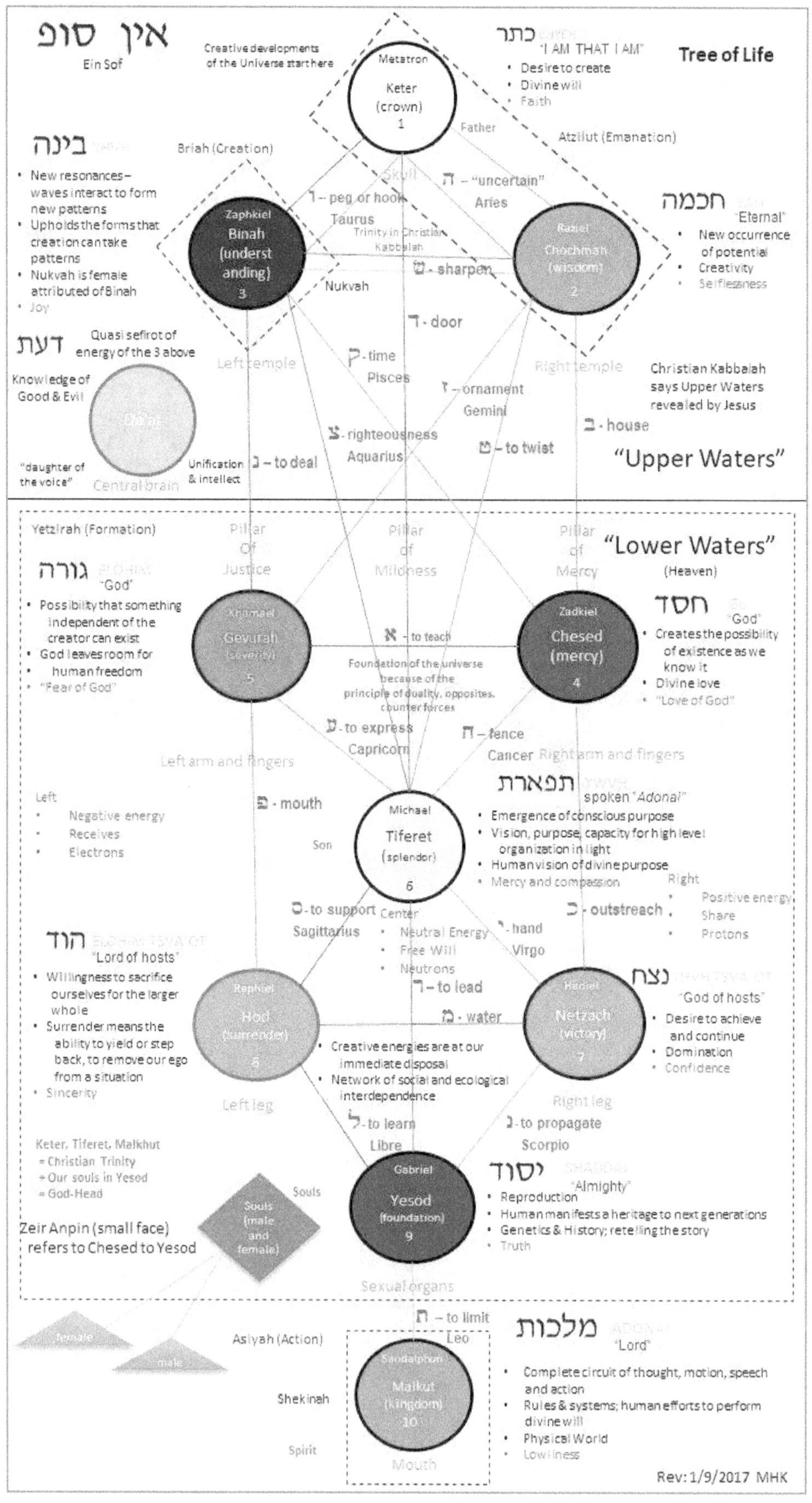

אין סוף
Ein Sof
Tree of Life
Creative developments of the Universe start here
כתר
"I AM THAT I AM"
Desire to create
Divine will
Faith
Metatron
Keter (crown)
1
Father
Atzilut (Emanation)
בינה
New resonances – waves interact to form new patterns
Upholds the forms that creation can take patterns
Nukvah is female attributed of Binah
Joy
Briah (Creation)
ה – "uncertain"
Aries
ו – peg or hook
Taurus
Trinity in Christian Kabbalah
Zaphkiel
Binah (understanding)
3
Raziel
Chochmah (wisdom)
2
חכמה
"Eternal"
New occurrence of potential
Creativity
Selflessness
ש – sharpen
Nukvah
ד - door
דעת
Quasi sefirot of energy of the 3 above
Knowledge of Good & Evil
"daughter of the voice"
Da'at
Central brain
Left temple
ק - time
Pisces
ז – ornament
Gemini
Right temple
ב - house
צ - righteousness
Aquarius
ט – to twist
Christian Kabbalah says Upper Waters revealed by Jesus
ג – to deal
Unification & intellect
"Upper Waters"
Yetzirah (Formation)
Pillar Of Justice
Pillar of Mildness
Pillar of Mercy
"Lower Waters"
(Heaven)
גורה
ELOHIM
"God"
Possibility that something independent of the creator can exist
God leaves room for human freedom
"Fear of God"
Khamael
Gevurah (severity)
5
א - to teach
Foundation of the universe because of the principle of duality, opposites, counter forces
Zadkiel
Chesed (mercy)
4
חסד
EL
"God"
Creates the possibility of existence as we know it
Divine love
"Love of God"
Left
Negative energy
Receives
Electrons
ע - to express
Capricorn
Left arm and fingers
ח – fence
Cancer Right arm and fingers
תפארת
YHWH
spoken Adonai
Emergence of conscious purpose
Vision, purpose, capacity for high level organization in light
Human vision of divine purpose
Mercy and compassion
פ - mouth
Michael
Tiferet (splendor)
6
Son
Right
Positive energy
Share
Protons
כ - to support Center
Sagittarius
Neutral Energy
Free Will
Neutrons
ד - outstreach
י - hand
Virgo
הוד
ELOHIM TSVA OT
"Lord of hosts"
Willingness to sacrifice ourselves for the larger whole
Surrender means the ability to yield or step back, to remove our ego from a situation
Sincerity
Raphiel
Hod (surrender)
8
ר - to lead
מ - water
Haniel
Netzach (victory)
7
נצח
YHWH TSVA OT
"God of hosts"
Desire to achieve and continue
Domination
Confidence
Creative energies are at our immediate disposal
Network of social and ecological interdependence
Left leg
Right leg
ל - to learn
Libre
נ - to propagate
Scorpio
Keter, Tiferet, Malkhut
= Christian Trinity
= Our souls in Yesod
= God-Head
Gabriel
Yesod (foundation)
9
יסוד
SHADDAI
"Almighty"
Reproduction
Human manifests a heritage to next generations
Genetics & History; retelling the story
Truth
Zeir Anpin (small face) refers to Chesed to Yesod
Souls (male and female)
Souls
Sexual organs
ת – to limit
Leo
מלכות
ADONAI
"Lord"
female
male
Asiyah (Action)
Shekinah
Spirit
Sandalphon
Malkut (kingdom)
10
Complete circuit of thought, motion, speech and action
Rules & systems; human efforts to perform divine will
Physical World
Lowliness
Mouth
Rev: 1/9/2017 MHK

114

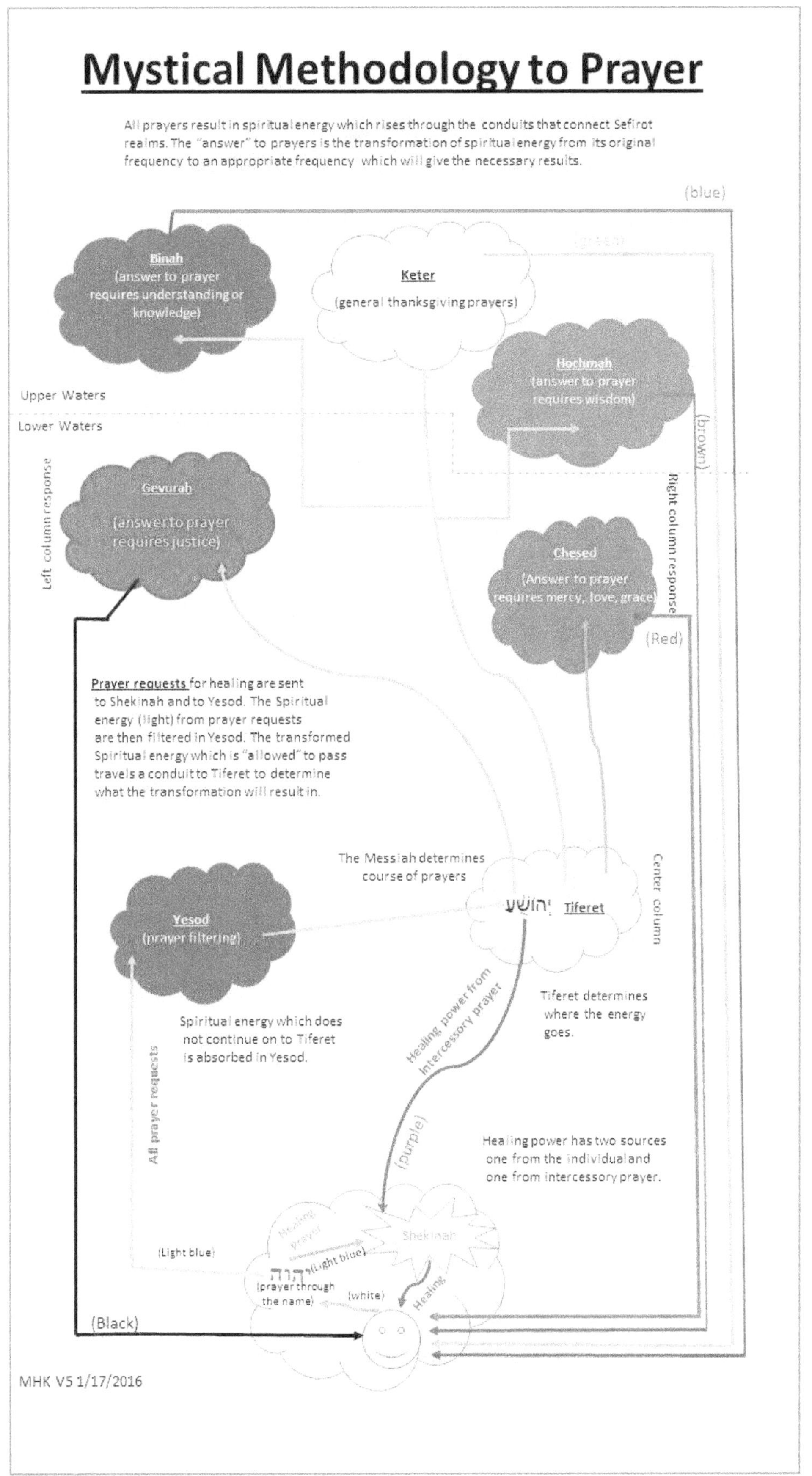

Mystical Methodology to Prayer

All prayers result in spiritual energy which rises through the conduits that connect Sefirot realms. The "answer" to prayers is the transformation of spiritual energy from its original frequency to an appropriate frequency which will give the necessary results.

(blue)
(green)

Binah
(answer to prayer requires understanding or knowledge)

Keter
(general thanksgiving prayers)

Hochmah
(answer to prayer requires wisdom)

Upper Waters
Lower Waters

(brown)

Gevurah
(answer to prayer requires justice)

Chesed
(Answer to prayer requires mercy, love, grace)

(Red)

Left column response

Right column response

Prayer requests for healing are sent to Shekinah and to Yesod. The Spiritual energy (light) from prayer requests are then filtered in Yesod. The transformed Spiritual energy which is "allowed" to pass travels a conduit to Tiferet to determine what the transformation will result in.

The Messiah determines course of prayers

יהושע Tiferet

Center column

Yesod
(prayer filtering)

Tiferet determines where the energy goes.

Spiritual energy which does not continue on to Tiferet is absorbed in Yesod.

Healing power from Intercessory prayer

All prayer requests

Healing power has two sources one from the individual and one from intercessory prayer.

(purple)

(Light blue)

Healing prayer

Shekinah

יהוה (light blue)
(prayer through the name)

(white)

Healing

(Black)

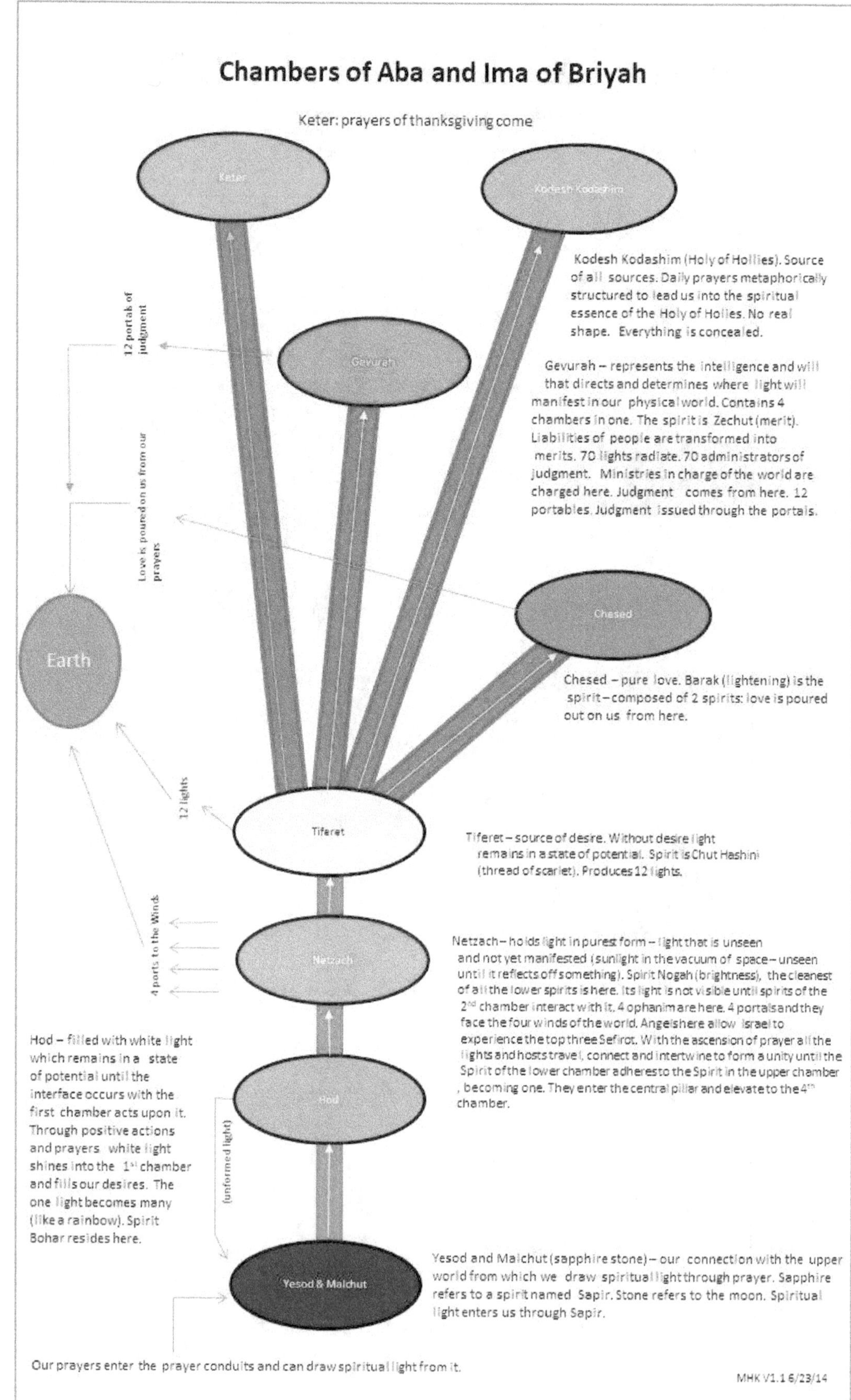

Chambers of Aba and Ima of Briyah
Keter: prayers of thanksgiving come
Keter
Kodesh Kodashim
Kodesh Kodashim (Holy of Hollies). Source of all sources. Daily prayers metaphorically structured to lead us into the spiritual essence of the Holy of Holies. No real shape. Everything is concealed.
Gevurah
Gevurah – represents the intelligence and will that directs and determines where light will manifest in our physical world. Contains 4 chambers in one. The spirit is Zechut (merit). Liabilities of people are transformed into merits. 70 lights radiate. 70 administrators of judgment. Ministries in charge of the world are charged here. Judgment comes from here. 12 portables. Judgment issued through the portals.
12 portals of judgment
Love is poured on us from our prayers
Earth
Chesed
Chesed – pure love. Barak (lightening) is the spirit – composed of 2 spirits: love is poured out on us from here.
12 lights
Tiferet
Tiferet – source of desire. Without desire light remains in a state of potential. Spirit is Chut Hashini (thread of scarlet). Produces 12 lights.
4 ports to the Winds
Netzach
Netzach – holds light in purest form – light that is unseen and not yet manifested (sunlight in the vacuum of space – unseen until it reflects off something). Spirit Nogah (brightness), the cleanest of all the lower spirits is here. Its light is not visible until spirits of the 2nd chamber interact with it. 4 ophanim are here. 4 portals and they face the four winds of the world. Angels here allow Israel to experience the top three Sefirot. With the ascension of prayer all the lights and hosts travel, connect and intertwine to form a unity until the Spirit of the lower chamber adhere to the Spirit in the upper chamber, becoming one. They enter the central pillar and elevate to the 4th chamber.
Hod
Hod – filled with white light which remains in a state of potential until the interface occurs with the first chamber acts upon it. Through positive actions and prayers white light shines into the 1st chamber and fills our desires. The one light becomes many (like a rainbow). Spirit Bohar resides here.
(unformed light)
Yesod & Malchut
Yesod and Malchut (sapphire stone) – our connection with the upper world from which we draw spiritual light through prayer. Sapphire refers to a spirit named Sapir. Stone refers to the moon. Spiritual light enters us through Sapir.
Our prayers enter the prayer conduits and can draw spiritual light from it.
MHK V1.1 6/23/14

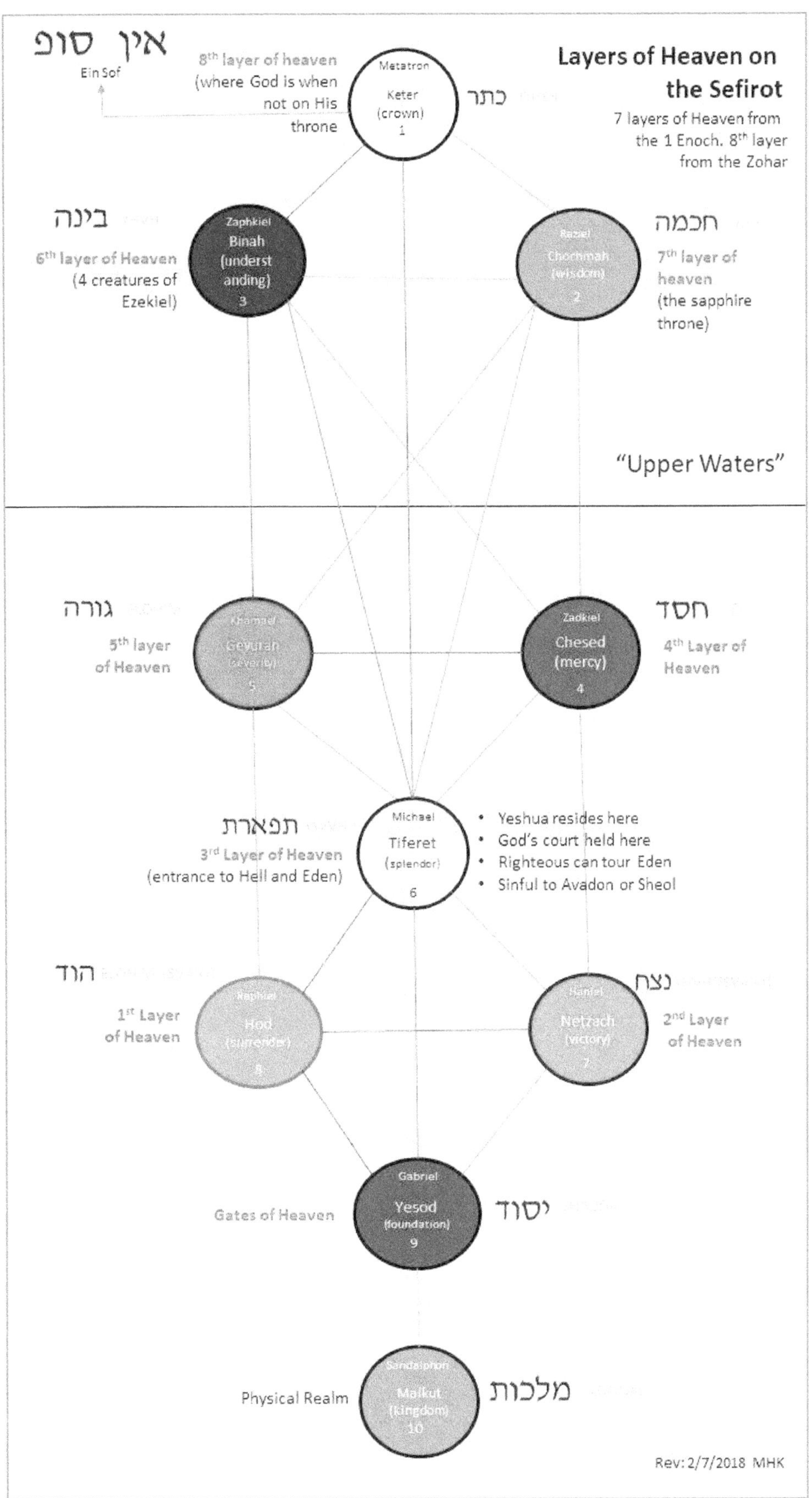
אין סוף
Ein Sof

8th layer of heaven
(where God is when
not on His
throne

Metatron
Keter
(crown)
1

כתר

Layers of Heaven on
the Sefirot

7 layers of Heaven from
the 1 Enoch. 8th layer
from the Zohar

בינה

6th layer of Heaven
(4 creatures of
Ezekiel)

Zaphkiel
Binah
(understanding)
3

חכמה

Raziel
Chochmah
(wisdom)
2

7th layer of
heaven
(the sapphire
throne)

"Upper Waters"

גורה

5th layer
of Heaven

Khamael
Gevurah
(severity)
5

Zadkiel
Chesed
(mercy)
4

חסד

4th Layer of
Heaven

תפארת

3rd Layer of Heaven
(entrance to Hell and Eden)

Michael
Tiferet
(splendor)
6

• Yeshua resides here
• God's court held here
• Righteous can tour Eden
• Sinful to Avadon or Sheol

הוד

1st Layer
of Heaven

Raphael
Hod
(surrender)
8

Haniel
Netzach
(victory)
7

נצח

2nd Layer
of Heaven

Gabriel
Yesod
(foundation)
9

יסוד

Gates of Heaven

Sandalphon
Malkut
(kingdom)
10

מלכות

Physical Realm

Rev: 2/7/2018 MHK